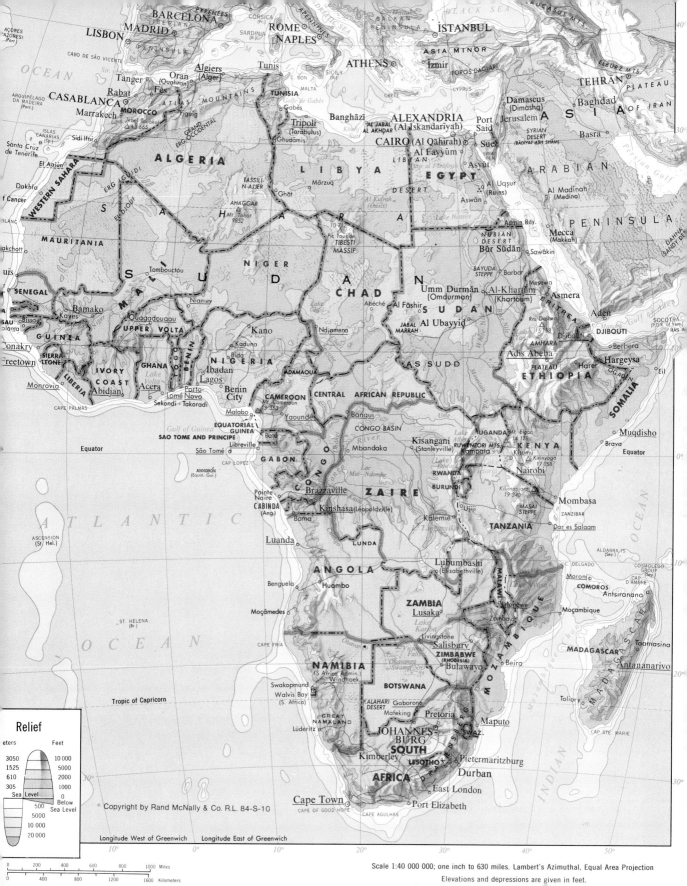

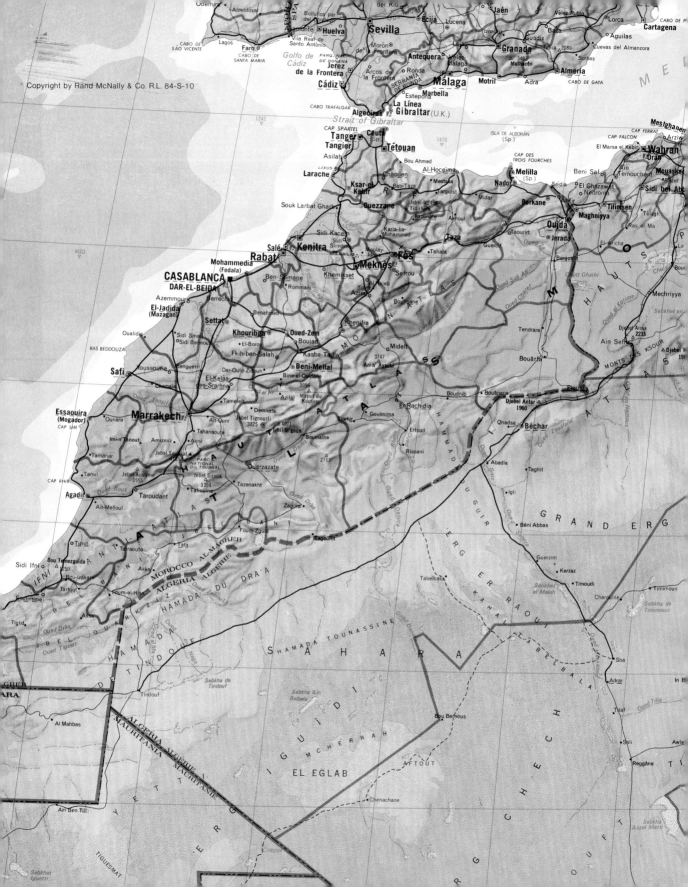

Enchantment of the World

MOROCCO

By Martin Hintz

Consultant: John P. Entelis, Ph.D., Department of Political Science, Fordham University, Bronx, New York

Consultant for Reading: Robert L. Hillerich, Ph.D., Bowling Green State University, Bowling Green, Ohio

CHILDRENS PRESS ™
CHICAGO

Schoolboys in Marrakech

To Dan, for all of his reaching

When more than one spelling exists for Arabic or Berber words, Childrens Press has chosen to use the common French usage. In the case of living people, proper names are spelled according to the person's preference.

Library of Congress Cataloging in Publication Data

Hintz, Martin.
  Morocco.

  (Enchantment of the world)
  Includes index.
  Summary: Presents the history, geography, natural history, economy, customs, and people of this diverse North African country.
  1. Morocco—Juvenile literature. [1. Morocco]
I. Title. II. Series.
DT305.H56 1985   964   84-23269
ISBN 0-516-02774-3

Picture Acknowledgments
Chip/Rosa Maria Peterson: Stephen Johnson: Pages 4, 6 (top), 59 (top), 61
Root Resources: © Ruth V. Welty: Pages 5, 62 (bottom right), 67 (left); © Russel A. Kriete: Pages 18, 48, 52 (top), 56, 60, 75 (left);   John Chitty: Pages 21 (left), 22, 25, 27 (left), 84 (bottom right); 86, 108;   Jane H. Kriete: Pages 26, 37, 55 (right), 58;   Grace H. Lanctot: Pages 69 (left), 84 (bottom left);   Florence Porter Turner: Pages 28 (top), 84 (top)
Victor Englebert: Pages 6 (bottom), 8, 9, 14, 16, 19, 20, 21 (right), 23, 28 (bottom), 62 (middle and bottom left), 69 (right), 73 (left), 77 (right), 87, 91, 94, 95, 101, 104 (2 photos), 107, 122 (bottom)
Chandler Forman: Pages 10, 12, 40, 52 (bottom), 62 (top), 75 (right), 79, 106
Nawrocki Stock Photo: Wm. S. Nawrocki: Pages 11, 31, 54, 59 (bottom), 65 (left), 66 (left), 70, 73 (right), 77 (left), 78, 81, 83, 88, 89, 90, 92, 96, 99 (2 photos), 100, 103, 105 (2 photos), 112 (top), 117, 122 (top)
Roloc Color Slides: Cover, Pages 13, 17, 27 (right), 30, 55 (left), 64, 65 (right), 66 (right), 67 (right), 68, 80
Historical Pictures Service, Chicago: Pages 32 (2 photos), 34, 35, 38, 43, 45 (left)
United Press International: Pages 45 (right), 46, 47, 49, 50
Tom Stack & Associates: B.J. Cogbill: Page 74
The Marilyn Gartman Agency: Robert Drea: Page 112 (bottom)
Courtesy Flag Research Center, Winchester, Massachusetts 01890: Flag on back cover
Cover: Rif Mountains

*The Gate of
the Saddlers
in Meknès*

TABLE OF CONTENTS

*Above: A market in
    Marrakech
Below: A snake charmer
    in the square
    of Jemaa-el-Fna
    in Marrakech.*

Chapter 1

OLD WAYS BLEND
TO NEW

Mustafa dashed through the crowd. The souk (market) was jammed. There was barely room for him to wriggle past the vendors in the open square of the medina, or old city. Their flimsy stalls were packed with anything anyone would ever want to buy. There were candy bars, dried figs, transistor radios, and *kesrah*, which is Moroccan bread. Mustafa paused to buy a biscuit and some mint tea. He laughed as the baker produced a pattern on the dough by pushing it against his belly button.

Dodging a snake charmer, Mustafa ran almost headlong into a doctor preparing a potion for a patient. The man yelled at Mustafa to be careful. The boy barely heard him over the clamor of the crowd. There was no time to lose. Youssef, his best friend, would be waiting for him. Youssef's father had a leather-work stall near the city's main gate. But a crunch like this during *Souk el Khemis*, the market of the fifth day (Thursday), would slow even the fastest runner.

A market outside the city walls of Marrakech

RAMADAN

It was also the thirtieth day of Ramadan, the ninth month of the Muslim calendar and the holiest time of the year. Everyone was buying food.

From dawn to sunset for the entire month of Ramadan, no adult Muslim can eat or drink, although water is allowed. Only sick people, pregnant women, the aged, and soldiers can break the fast. Ramadan commemorates the first revelation of the Koran, the Muslim holy book. In that ancient volume, God told the Prophet Muhammad how to lead a good life.

But now the new moon was sighted. The fasting was over. It was time for the festival of Aïd es Séghir! Tomorrow, on the plains outside of the city, the Berbers would honor the birthday of the Prophet with the traditional fantasia, the charge of the horsemen. Mustafa could hardly wait to see the spirited war-horses wearing their fanciest breast bands and tassels. White-turbaned riders would form a platoon at one end of the field. They would then charge at a gallop toward the crush of onlookers.

Horsemen show their skill in the fantasia.

At the last second, as everyone shouted and cheered, the riders would rein in their mounts amid a choking cloud of dust. All the riders would stand in their stirrups and fire their guns into the air. It would be quite a sight, one that Mustafa and Youssef eagerly awaited each year.

But that was tomorrow. And Youssef was waiting now. So Mustafa kept running, his bright new *djellaba,* a hooded robe, swishing about his legs. There would be dancing tonight outside the walls of the Casbah, the citadel in the center of town.

Fires would be lighted in hundreds of braziers. These little metal pans held burning charcoal for warmth and light in the Moroccan dusk.

Already, Mustafa could hear the tambourine players and the strolling minstrels with their flutes, improvising songs. Then the drums started their thumping and the *gimbris,* Moroccan violins, began their scraping melodies.

A leather stall selling purses, luggage, and slippers

Overhead, a flock of startled storks soared past the minaret, the tower of the mosque where the muezzin calls faithful Muslims to communal prayer five times a day. Actually clumsy scavengers, the storks were graceful in flight as they beat their heavy wings against the tired evening air. Associated with the spirits of the dead, the birds were allowed to fly free.

Youssef was waiting near his father's stall, where the scent of rich new leather was like a perfume. The two boys were hungry for the spicy little sausages broiled on long skewers over open fires. They could hardly wait to dig into dishes of delicious chick-pea paste. Old Chedlya, who set up her stall near the well, always made the best.

Women dancing the ahouache

THE SOUK

It was exciting in the souk. Everyone wore their best clothes.
Fathers carried children on their shoulders. Veiled women flowed
through the crowd, elegant in bright caftans.

Mustafa and Youssef gaped at the storytellers, the magicians,
the monkey trainers, the Chleuh dancers. Somehow, in the
growing night, everything became bigger than life, lighted by
torches and braziers.

The *ahouache* — a dance — was already beginning, the girls lining
up in a circle near the center of the crowd.

As the tambourines and drums beat out a wild rhythm, the
dancers rolled their heads and began swaying and chanting to the
music. The pace quickened and the dancers circled to the right,
their shuffling feet masking the intricate steps. Hands hung at
their sides and faces stared straight ahead, the line split, one part
going to the left and the other continuing right. They circled until
they came face to face.

Eventually, the music slowed and the dancers stopped. The

Berber musicians and dancers

musicians stood up to collect tossed coins. The crowd drifted on to
another part of the market where there was more dancing.

The two boys spent the next few hours wandering around the
souk, eating honey cakes and drinking mint tea. Whenever they
grew tired, they simply sat to one side to listen and watch. Then it
was time for home and bed.

OLD AND NEW

The next morning at dawn, Mustafa and Youssef awakened to
the cry of the muezzin, high in his tower. A Royal Air Maroc jet
from Paris flew overhead, heading for the international airport at
Casablanca, one of Morocco's principal cities. Neither boy took
any notice. After last night's excitement, it was all they could do
to struggle out of their beds.

*A street scene in Tangier shows people dressed
in traditional clothes and Western dress.*

In Morocco, the old ways coexist with the modern. Moroccans seem to take it all in stride, keeping their wonderful traditions while living in a twentieth-century world.

Morocco is a country surprising for its diversity. It is not all desert and oasis, although the mighty Sahara forms its southern boundary. This provides an effective 1,000-mile-wide (1,609-kilometer) barrier of sand. But inland from the Mediterranean Sea (the northern border) and from the Atlantic Ocean (the western edge), Morocco has rich agricultural fields. The country's major cities are there as well, a colorful blend of donkeys and trucks, of robes and business suits, of veiled women and discos.

Morocco is a country finding its own place in the hubbub of today's world. It stays aware of its past through custom and religion. Yet Morocco is a leader of the northern African community, with its people open, warm, and friendly.

In winter the Atlas Mountains are frequently covered with snow.

Chapter 2

THE SURPRISING LAND

The Kingdom of Morocco (in Arabic, "al-Mamlakat al-Maghribiya") is on the rim of North Africa, which is called *El Maghreb el Aksa.* This can mean either "Land of the Setting Sun" or "Land Farthest West" in Arabic. Although it has the windswept and desolate Sahara desert for a southern border, much of the country is very fertile. Sometimes there is so much winter snow in the mountains that plows are needed day after day to keep the roads open. Floods are very frequent in the spring. Some parts of Morocco receive 40 inches (1,016 millimeters) of rain a year.

Morocco was given its name by European mapmakers in the seventeenth century. Originally, the term was applied only to the countryside around Marrakech, one of the principal cities of the region. The rest of the land was divided into two other kingdoms, with capitals in Fès and Tafilalet. Morocco did not become a unified, independent nation until 1956.

It is possible to divide Morocco into several geographical

The Dades Valley in the Atlas Mountains

regions. Mountains run across Morocco from northeast to southwest, marking off the fertile north from the land abutting the Sahara. The geography of each region is different.

Moving from west to east, first come the flat plains, then the Rif Mountains. After these are the Sebou and Innaouen plateaus. The 450-mile-long (724-kilometer) Atlas Mountain range is next, which includes Djebel Toubkal, the highest peak in North Africa, at 13,665 feet (4,165 meters) above sea level.

Moving eastward and to the south is the *hammada*, a rocky, desert area that has to be crossed before reaching the sands of the Sahara. Eastern Morocco is the large area between the Middle Atlas Mountains and Algeria, the country's neighbor. This is mostly a level plateau.

A water hole on the road from Casablanca to Marrakech

LAND BORDERS

Morocco's land borders do not follow natural boundaries, such as rivers or mountain ranges. This has often caused conflict with Algeria on the east and Mauritania on the south. Most of these problems were resolved by the early 1980s. There is still fighting, however, over who owns what on the western edges of the Sahara. The former Spanish Sahara was divided by Morocco and Mauritania in 1976. Since Mauritania's withdrawal in August 1979, Morocco now administers the entire territory. The United Nations, the Organization of African Unity, and other legal international bodies do not recognize the annexation. They call the region Western Sahara. The Polisario rebels from that region want to form their own country. It is also difficult to enforce territorial laws because many of the border people are nomads who travel a great deal. They are inclined to ignore frontiers as

Essaouira, a city on the Atlantic coast

they follow their flocks and herds.

The northern and western borders are easy to determine, however. On the west is the Atlantic Ocean, with 612 miles (985 kilometers) of shoreline from the Strait of Gibraltar to Western Sahara. To the north is the Mediterranean Sea, with 234 miles (377 kilometers) of shoreline from Gibraltar to Algeria.

Beautiful beaches along both coasts are popular with tourists from around the world. The Strait of Gibraltar, which connects the Atlantic with the Mediterranean, is nine miles (fourteen kilometers) wide from Morocco to Tarifa, Spain.

Few hardy Moroccans who live along the coast make their living from the sea. The offshore waters are very treacherous. The undertow and the rocks make swimming dangerous at many points. Yet these same dangers protected Morocco from invasions for centuries.

A fortified Berber village in the Atlas Mountains

Morocco itself has an area of 254,816 square miles (659,970 square kilometers). Most of the population lives in the north, between the Rif and Atlas mountains, where the best land can be cultivated. The major cities are here as well. Oases dot the desert land to the south. Travelers can still see *ksour,* the fortified villages of the Berbers.

The Dra River, which is often dry, empties into the Atlantic Ocean.

It seems as if every town in Morocco has some tie to the past. Even out-of-the way places such as Agadir on the Atlantic coast have been caught up by historic events. It lies on the bay at the mouth of the Oued Sous River. For centuries, it had been invaded, burned, and rebuilt. Invaders could easily beach their boats. Even nature seemed not to like Agadir. An earthquake in 1960 killed thousands of people there. The ruins of the old city were left as a memorial to the dead and a new city built nearby. It is much more calm now, becoming a tourist center.

Morocco has several major rivers, important for irrigation of crops. The Moulouya empties into the Mediterranean and the Loukkos pours into the Atlantic. Others include the Sebou, the Grou, the Bou Regreg, and the Oum er Rbia. There are even some rivers just north of the Sahara, such as the Ziz and the Dades, which flow southward out of the Atlas Mountains. As you can imagine, by the time they get to the *hammada*, the fringes of the desert, there isn't much water left.

WINTERS AND WINDS

The climate is very pleasant in western and northern Morocco. But the mountains prevent the ocean wind from air conditioning

In the Rif (left) and Atlas (right) mountains, winter snows are often quite heavy.

the interior of Morocco in the summer. It can become very cold in the mountains during the winter, sometimes hitting the below-zero mark.

The western slopes of the mountains are covered with fir trees and other vegetation. Little rain or snow is carried over to the eastern side because of the height of the mountains.

Winters can be cold and stormy, with lots of snow. It is hot and dry in the summer except in the mountains, where mighty rainstorms can be triggered in June or July. No matter where they live, Moroccans dread the middle of summer when the siroccos, sometimes called the *chergui*, occasionally roar in from the Sahara. These are hot and very dry winds that bring choking clouds of dust. The siroccos seem to find every crack in the mountains, sneaking through to hit the seacoasts as well as the inland cities.

Moroccan tourist officials boast that they can promise three hundred days of sunshine a year for visitors. Usually they are correct.

Date palms grow in Zagora, which borders on the desert.

There are very few lakes in Morocco, except those produced by the damming of rivers.

Morocco has a very thin level of soil, but dwarf palm trees and grass cover northern Morocco like a green carpet. Vegetation thins out as the desert approaches.

Only date palms and a few hardy bushes can be found in the oases, which are irrigated by wells. There is an ancient folk saying that claims the palm "grows with its feet in the water and its head in the fire." Hardly any other plants survive the harsh climate and the towering sand dunes of the Sahara.

Goats climb an argan tree to eat the juicy leaves.

There is a wide variety of plants in the mountains. However, many areas are barren because of wild goats that seem to eat everything in sight. Cedar trees, cork oaks, and olive trees are abundant. There are even some pine trees in the Rif. In the Atlas grows the thuja tree, which looks something like a cypress. Along the riverbanks are elm and ash trees.

The carob tree grows throughout Morocco. Its seeds cannot be eaten, but North African jewelers in ancient times used them as weights to measure treasures. The word *carat* as a measurement for precious gems comes from the Arabic word *karab* or *carob*.

Don't be surprised if you see a goat in a tree in Morocco. These hardy animals love the fruit of the argan. Although the trees prickle with thorns, the goats scamper up into the branches to munch the juicy leaves. Moroccans use oil derived from argan fruit for frying foods.

ANIMAL LIFE

Few large wild animals gallop across the Moroccan landscape, but rabbits seem to be leaping everywhere. Of course, that makes the striped hyenas, foxes, and jackals happy. They are the largest meat-eating animals in the country and are found mostly in the east. The Moroccans use ferrets, weasellike animals, to hunt rabbits, which often damage crops.

Wild boars also create trouble when they rummage through small mountain gardens. A popular sport is to hunt and kill them. Their hides are sold to leather workers and their tusks used for magic.

Rare Barbary apes live in the foothills of the Rif Mountains, as do porcupines and hedgehogs. A large colony of the apes lives in Gibraltar, just across the strait from Morocco. They are the only wild monkeys living in Europe. Barbary sheep, with their huge curving horns, can be spotted leaping from cliff to cliff in the Atlas Mountains.

There are many birds in Morocco. White vultures, hawks, eagles, and owls help control the rodent population in the countryside. Pigeons and other birds that are good for eating are everywhere. So are sparrows and ravens.

Snakes are not very common in Morocco. However, in the south there are some poisonous species, such as the puff adder and Egyptian cobra.

"SHIPS OF THE DESERT"

In prehistory days, giraffes, elephants, lions, crocodiles, and hippopotamuses lived in Morocco. They disappeared eons ago,

Part of a camel caravan

Every summer a camel market is held in Goulimine.

probably as the climate changed and the human population increased. The camel was not introduced to Morocco until the fourth century A.D. It is a very versatile animal and is used by the natives for hauling goods and for riding. Most cities have camel markets in which breeders display and sell their animals.

Camels are perfectly adapted to the Moroccan landscape. They have thick pads on their knees and chests that protect them when sleeping on the rocky ground. Their broad, padded feet enable them to cross the sand dunes. A camel can go for several days without drinking water, and for a longer period if edible plants are available. Moisture in the plants is enough for a thirsty camel. A strong camel can carry from 500 to 600 pounds (227 to 272 kilograms) and travel up to 30 miles (48 kilometers) a day.

Many of the Berbers and the Tulags, two Moroccan tribes, breed racing and fighting camels. These are more slender than the freight-hauling "ships of the desert." Camels fight with their

Left: *An annual camel race is held at Tan Tan.*
Right: *The Moroccans are proud of their fine horses.*

teeth, some of which are sharply pointed. They can be very mean. Imagine cramming hundreds of the ornery creatures into a large courtyard. Think of all the bellowing, the shouts of the sellers, the camel smells and droppings. That's a camel market!

Camel drivers don't like the cities. They prefer the open spaces. One guidebook calls the Sahara the world's largest camping ground. Camels seem to like the vast stretch of rock and sand just as well. But it's hard to tell with camels. They are usually so grumpy.

Moroccans love horses. Desert tribes will often wager their best animals in a race. It is a point of honor to have a fine string of horses.

There is the legend of the great Muslim warrior, Oqba ben Nafi, who rode his horse into the Atlantic Ocean. He wanted to show Allah that he had finally conquered all of Morocco. Like its master, the brave horse was not afraid of the waves.

Left: Berber women on
    their way to the souk
Below: A storyteller
    attracts quite a
    crowd in Jemaa el Fna
    Square in Marrakech.

Chapter 3

OUT OF THE PAST

___

THE BERBERS: FREE MEN

For thousands of years, people have lived in Morocco. However, little trace of the land's earliest inhabitants has ever been found except for some cave paintings high in the Atlas Mountains. But since recorded history, one race has been predominant.

These are Berbers, still the major ethnic population of Morocco. No one seems to know their origin. Some scholars think they are descendants of ancient Libyans, another North African people. Their architecture is similar to that found in Egypt. Their art resembles that of areas even farther east. Possibly the Berbers came to Morocco by following the Mediterranean coast, halting when they arrived at the Atlantic.

The Berbers had neither an alphabet nor a written language. Their history was handed down by storytellers. The tales became very colorful over the generations. Eventually, the true story about their origin was lost.

The Berbers never had a name for themselves, preferring to be

The remains of a Phoenician city on the coast near Tangier

known only as *imazighan,* or free men. Early Europeans first identified all Moroccans as Berbers. Later, in medieval times, Moroccans were called Moors. The Berbers didn't think in terms of "nation" in that dim past. They looked to the family and tribe as being most important. They were independent, roaming wherever they wished between the Rif and Atlas mountains.

Phoenician traders in the twelfth century B.C. were among the first outsiders to visit the land that would become Morocco. They founded a seaport at Tangier and built other harbors that would eventually become Morocco's most important cities. After the Phoenicians came the Carthaginians. Both of these peoples were primarily traders. They were friendly with the Berbers. One ancient Carthaginian explorer, Hanno, described his adventures along the coast of Morocco. It is one of the first historical accounts of the region.

Roman ruins of the former capital of North Africa, Tingis

THE ROMANS: A COLONY

The Carthaginians were conquered by the Romans by 146 B.C. Soon, the Roman Empire was firmly entrenched over much of the Mediterranean world.

For two hundred years, the Romans ruled Morocco, calling the province Mauretania Tingitana. The name meant "Land of the Maures," or Moors, from which the European word *Morocco* originated. The capital of the district was Tangier. However, the Romans changed the name of the city to Tingis.

Rome's Emperor Augustus knew the value of keeping Morocco as a colony. With influence in both Spain and Morocco, the Romans could control the Strait of Gibraltar and all the trade that passed through it. Juba II, a Berber king, was appointed as ruler of

Caligula (left) was one of the Roman emperors who ruled Morocco until the Vandals and the Goths (right) drove them out in the fifth century.

Morocco. He married the daughter of the Roman general Marc Antony and Egypt's Queen Cleopatra. Under his reign, Morocco prospered.

Yet the next Roman emperor, Caligula, was afraid that Juba's successors would rebel against him. So he put Morocco directly under Roman rule. Caligula also divided the kingdom of Morocco into two provinces to keep the Berbers from becoming too strong.

THE BERBERS: A SCHISM

By the third century after Christ, the Romans were in trouble at home. They were attacked by fierce barbarians storming into their homeland of Italy from northern Europe.

They pulled most of their troops out of Africa, keeping fortifications only at a small area around Tingis (Tangier). The

Berbers took advantage of the plight of the Romans by attacking their outposts. In addition, years earlier, some Berbers had given up their pagan religion to become Christians. They did this primarily as another means of "attacking" the Romans, who also were pagans.

When the Roman Empire eventually adopted Christianity as its state religion, the Berbers protested again. Many split away from the European church. This division was called a schism. The Berbers resented any outsiders telling them what to do. The schism was simply another form of rebellion.

Goths and Vandals from Germany eventually overran Roman Spain and parts of North Africa. It was simple for them to build ships and sail across the narrow Strait of Gibraltar. By A.D. 429, the Roman authority was destroyed in Morocco—a victim of Berber protest and attacks by the invaders. The Byzantine Empire, which followed on the heels of the Romans, attempted to regain authority. It failed.

At this time, the Berbers consisted of three major tribes: the Masmoudas, the Sanhajas, and the Zenata. The Masmoudas lived along the northern coast and in the Atlas Mountains. Most were farmers. The Sanhajas were warlike nomads who ranged deep into Africa as far south as the black kingdom of Senegal. The Sanhajas were excellent camel riders. They were nicknamed the Veiled Men because of headcloths worn as shields from the desert sun. The Zenatas, however, preferred horses and were excellent cavalrymen. They lived in eastern Morocco.

Over the centuries, as the influence of outsiders decreased, these three tribes battled for power in Morocco. There was constant warfare.

Arab desert warriors

THE MUSLIMS: CONQUERORS

In the 600s and 700s, a major change swept across North Africa. It came in the form of religion. All traces of Christianity and European influence disappeared. Mounted Arab warriors, called Muslims, charged out of the east. They were intent on conquering the world in the name of Allah, the Arabic name for God. The Muslims followed the teachings of the Prophet Muhammad.

Muhammad lived in the Arabian town of Mecca. He preached against the paganism of the people around him. Eventually he and his followers were driven away. This was called "the flight;" or the "hegira," which marks the beginning of the Muslim (or Islamic) calendar. According to the European calendar, this was in the year A.D. 622. Muhammad built up an army and eventually defeated his enemies. He died in A.D. 632.

After his death, his followers put Muhammad's thoughts and philosophies into a book called the Koran, which is as important

A portion of the Koran, the Muslims' sacred book

to Muslims as the Bible is to Christians. The Koran is the Muslims' guide to everything that must be done during life. The word *Islam* means "submission to God" in Arabic. Therefore, a person who "submits" belongs to the Islamic (or Muslim) faith.

The Muslims developed a powerful military machine that they used to spread their religion. Before a battle, they would shout, "There is no god but Allah and Muhammad is His Prophet."

The first Muslim raids into Morocco date from 682 to 683. For twenty-five years, the Berbers resisted the attacks. In 701, Arab armies—vast columns of men on horses and camels—roared across eastern Morocco and through the mountain passes. They were led by Moussa ibn Nusair. It did not take long before most of Morocco was subdued.

The Muslims were so successful that they decided to attack Spain. Many of the newly converted Berbers joined the Arab forces and helped conquer Andalusia, a province in southern

Spain. The Moorish or Moroccan influence in art and architecture can still be seen there.

The Koran said that all Muslims were to be treated equally. However, the Omayyad caliphs (the Arab military governors) were very strict. They taxed the Berbers heavily. Naturally, the Berbers objected and felt the Arabs were unfair.

Once again, the Berbers split away. It was another schism, similar to those during Roman and Christian times. The Berbers joined the Kharidjite rebels. They said that the caliphs should be elected from among qualified Muslims instead of being Arabs who were descendants of Muhammad. The Arabs called this heresy and put down the revolt. But they were never able to regain the same amount of control over the Berbers.

THE MOORS: SPANISH MUSLIMS

The Berbers attacked Spain again. They established themselves in the city of Cordoba, which became a center of learning and education in the Middle Ages. In Spain, the Berber Muslims were called Moors.

During this time, two other Muslim sects—the Sunni and the Shia—were fighting for control of Islam and the territory held by its warriors. The leader of the Shias, Idris ibn Abdallah, fled to Morocco when he was defeated by the Sunni.

Ibn Abdallah was the great-great-grandson of Ali, the son-in-law of Muhammad. He became *sharif*, a ruler directly descended from the Prophet. In 808, Idris ibn Abdallah founded the great city of Fès. His line remained in power from 788 to 974. Many aristocratic families in Fès can trace their lineage back to Idris ibn Abdallah and his son Idris II.

The three major tribes in Morocco, although now all Muslims,

Koutoubia Minaret was built by the Almoravids in the eleventh century.

still were not friendly with each other. The old rivalries did not die. Each supported different factions in the Muslim religious movement. This certainly did not encourage peace. The Sanhaja Berbers, who lived at the edge of the Sahara, became followers of a tiny group of Islamic monks called the Almoravids. They followed the Sunni philosophy. They wanted to purify the Muslim religion and put an end to all disputes.

Under the leadership of Youssef ben Tachfin, the Almoravids and the Sanhajas set out to conquer Morocco and much of the rest

El Cid, one of Spain's national heroes, helped to repel the Muslims.

of North Africa. Ben Tachfin built the first mosque in Marrakech, which was founded around 1062.

By 1082, the unification of Morocco was complete. In 1085, the Muslim princes in Spain asked for help against the Christians. The Spanish king, Alphonso, had established a policy of *reconquista* (reconquest) by which he hoped the Muslims would be pushed back into North Africa.

Youssef ben Tachfin himself led the Almoravid army across the Strait of Gibraltar into Spain. At first, he defeated the Spanish. Then he came up against the Spanish army led by General Rodrigo Díaz de Vivar, who was nicknamed "El Cid" ("The Sword"). El Cid eventually was able to push back the Muslims after many bloody battles.

THE BERBERS: THE LAST EMPIRE

For the next fifty years the Moorish-Muslim influence was at its
peak. But along came another reformer, Muhammad ibn Tumart,
who arrived at Marrakech and preached revolt. He said that the
Almoravids had forgotten the principles of Islam as they became
more powerful and rich. Ibn Tumart called himself the "mahdi,"
or Allah's envoy. Under his direction, his followers—who were
primarily Masmouda Berbers—eventually captured all of
Morocco. They were called the "Almohads."

Their rule lasted until 1269, when they were finally driven from
power by Zenata tribesmen of the Merinides dynasty. This third
great Berber empire lasted until the 1600s. But the power of the
Christian Europeans was growing at the same time. King
Ferdinand and Queen Isabella finally drove the remaining Moors
from Spain.

Thousands of Spanish Muslims, called the Moriscos, fled to
Morocco. The Spanish also drove out Jews, most of whom settled
in Morocco. The descendants of the Moriscos and the Jews
eventually became very powerful in government, banking, and
business.

The Spanish and the Portuguese carried their own form of holy
war to Morocco, capturing Tangier and other northern ports. They
also built some forts along the Atlantic coast but were unable to
hold them.

From that time on, Morocco was exposed to attacks from all
sides, as well as to turmoil within the country itself.

*The Saadian Tombs in Marrakech, built in the sixteenth century,
contain the remains of all but five of the Saadian rulers.*

Chapter 4

FORGING A NEW NATION

Morocco could not seem to find any peace in the sixteenth and seventeenth centuries. Muslims fought Muslims, Berbers fought Arabs, and everyone fought the Christian Europeans. Nothing seemed to go well. The rulers of Morocco came and went as swiftly as the flowing desert sand. There were several dynasties that rose and fell: The Merinides, the Bani Wattas, and the Saadians were families who attempted to seize and keep power.

Gold and slaves were brought by caravans across the Sahara from southern Africa. Marrakech, Fès, Agadir, and Safi glittered with new wealth. The Moroccan empire stretched from the Atlantic Ocean, across North Africa, and into the Sudan and Nigeria. It extended deep into black Africa. A leader of the Saadians, Sultan Ahmed el Mansour, established a Turkish form of government throughout his lands.

His system of pashas, or local governors, seemed to work very well at first. The tribes who supplied him with troops were exempt from taxation. Naturally, the sultan never had to worry about filling the ranks of his armies. These were called the *guich*, the Arabic word for army. The term eventually applied to all these special soldiers.

A SULTAN OF POWER

As the years rolled on, the pashas lost power outside the major cities. Although the nobles were very rich, the ordinary Moroccans remained poor. It was time for another reformer.

Around the southern oases near the Sahara, an Arab tribe called the Alaouites was ready to take up the cause. About 1660, the Alaouites attacked under Moulay Rashid. He was followed by Moulay Ismail, who became sultan in 1672.

This man brought in fifty thousand black slaves to serve as soldiers in his mighty armies. Many of the slaves were eventually freed and married Berber and Arab women. Today, their descendants are one of the major ethnic strains in Morocco. In addition to the blacks, European soldiers of fortune also joined Moulay Ismail. They showed him how to improve the sailing and fighting abilities of his navy and how to construct fortifications.

This force was able to put down most of the rebellions by minor tribes. When the soldiers were not fighting, Moulay Ismail had them building the Casbahs.

Moulay Ismail wanted Morocco to stay in touch with Europe. He realized the trade advantages. He even sent envoys to most of the kings in Europe. When he died, his successors signed treaties with Denmark, Sweden, and other trade-oriented, commercial countries.

Yet the sultans who came after Moulay Ismail did not have his

A nineteenth-century illustration showing a battle scene of the Barbary Wars

power. They were unable to control the pirates who raided commerce along the North African shore. Allied with chiefs from Algeria and Tunisia, these pirates captured Christian ships and enslaved their crews.

In the 1780s, the United States even paid these chiefs an annual tribute of $10,000 to leave Yankee ships alone. The pirates accepted the money with a smile and went back to raiding. This resulted in the Barbary Wars, which ran from 1801 to 1805, with more fighting in 1815. Eventually, the pirates were defeated.

A THREAT FROM EUROPE

Great Britain, France, and Germany were busy colonizing Africa as the nineteenth century began. No one wanted to see Morocco fall into other hands. The British already held Gibraltar on the Spanish coast. They were worried that some other country would gain control of the Moroccan shore and block off the Mediterranean.

In 1830, France seized Algeria, Morocco's neighbor, and colonized it. Rebels fled to eastern Morocco, where they continued to attack the French. The French retaliated by bombarding Tangier, convincing the Moroccans not to help the Algerians.

By 1871, Algeria was subdued. The French turned their eyes on Morocco. But a conference of European powers decided that Morocco should be kept neutral. This did not deter the French for very long.

There were too many rivalries among the Moroccans. No single ruler could stand up to pressures from outside countries. There were many border disputes with French Algeria, which led to the occupation of some Moroccan territory by the French.

In 1906, another European conference sought to help settle the problems. Instead of protecting Morocco, it opened the door to more intervention by the French and the Spanish. The Moroccans were caught in the middle.

A COLONY OF FRANCE

The French and Spanish signed their own treaty, which allowed both powers control over certain territories and cities in Morocco. In 1912, Tangier was made an international zone, in which foreign dealings were to be handled by the French. The Muslim sultan was to be only a religious figurehead.

The Moroccans ran the day-to-day operations in their country. But the French assigned Marshal Louis Lyautey as governor-general to keep control of things. For the next few years, the French were busy pacifying the tribes who objected to the outsiders. However, during World War I, many Moroccan soldiers fought for the French in Europe.

Left: Marshal Louis Lyautey was appointed governor-general by the French.
Right: Abd-El-Krim, a Rif leader, surrendered to the French in 1926.

In the 1920s the bloody Rif War exploded. Moroccan nationalists hid in the mountains and raided French convoys. The French sent more than 300,000 men with tanks and planes to put down the rebellion. The Spanish added another 100,000. The Moroccans fought bravely but were defeated. By 1934, all areas within the borders of today's Morocco were finally quiet.

A SULTAN OF DISTINCTION

In 1927 a new sultan took over. He was Sidi Muhammad ben Youssef, a wise and patient ruler who did the best he could. Through his efforts Morocco eventually became more or less

*The Sultan of Morocco and President Paul Doumer
of France met in Paris in August of 1931.*

peaceful. However, there were still many nationalists who wanted
Morocco to be more independent. There were many disturbances.
Yet ben Youssef went ahead with his work, promoting agriculture,
mining, and commerce. Many public improvements were built—
roads, sewers, and post offices.

When France was overrun by Germany in World War II, ben
Youssef took in many refugees. He protected the Jewish
population although he was often threatened by the Germans,
who wanted to send the Moroccan Jews to concentration camps.
As the war ground on, Moroccans fought alongside the Allies to
help liberate Europe.

After the war the nationalists grew stronger. A new French
governor-general was very strict. He and the sultan often argued.
There were many riots. In August of 1953 the situation worsened.
The sultan, in his capital at Rabat, refused to sign over his power
to the French. The governor-general then deposed ben Youssef
and sent him into exile.

Moroccans celebrated when they learned that ben Youssef would be released from exile.

A new sultan was named. But he was not liked by the majority of Moroccans, who objected to the way he had been put on the throne. A civil war broke out, with terrorists on both sides causing much suffering. In 1955, the French gave up. They decided to bring ben Youssef back from exile.

On October 30, 1955, the French-supported sultan resigned and a council was named to run Morocco until the return of ben Youssef. He arrived in triumph on November 2 and took the name of Sultan Muhammad V.

THE SON OF A KING

On March 2, 1956, Morocco achieved its political independence from France. Muhammad V changed his title to that of king in 1957, saying it was important to keep up with the times. He instituted many governmental reforms before his death in 1961.

His son, Prince Moulay Hassan, was the next king. He took the name of Hassan II. The young ruler drew up a new constitution

The tomb of King Muhammad V in Rabat

for Morocco that gave equal rights to everyone, including women. Some traditionalists did not approve of this and they attempted to assassinate the king. They were unsuccessful and King Hassan II went on to make more changes. In 1963, he opened the first Moroccan parliament.

Morocco did not remain totally quiet. A border war with Algeria broke out but was resolved through the mediation of other African leaders. In 1965 student-led riots racked Casablanca. The protesters objected to a ruling by the government that all students were to receive some technical training. The young people were afraid this was designed to keep them from getting jobs in other professions. The crisis ended when King Hassan II took over all the legislative and executive power in the government and named himself as prime minister.

Hassan II supported the writing of a new constitution that was approved in March 1972. The document lessened the king's power and allowed the people more voice in their country's affairs. However, Hassan II remained head of state.

There were two more assassination attempts against the king in the summers of 1971 and 1972, both of which failed. Hassan was uninjured and went on to initiate more reforms. He was still king in the mid-1980s.

King Hassan II when he was three years old

A GOVERNMENT BY ROYALTY

Under the constitution, the king is both governmental and religious ruler. He appoints a Council of Ministers that consists of the prime minister and other cabinet officials who head the various departments. The king can initiate laws and send them to parliament. He is commander in chief of the armed forces and makes all military and civil appointments. The king is still very powerful.

King Hassan II was born on July 9, 1929, in Rabat. His father, Muhammad V, carefully prepared him to be his successor. As a young man Hassan was given many responsibilities. He could speak Arabic and French and was graduated with honors from the university. He has several higher degrees and studied law at the University of Bordeaux, France. Hassan was his father's principal adviser and commander in chief of the Moroccan armed forces for several years before Muhammad died. Hassan became king when

In 1961, shortly after becoming king, Hassan II (center), met with President Habib Bourguiba of Tunisia (left) and Algerian rebel leader Ferhat Abbas (right).

he was only thirty-two years old. He is the twenty-first king of the Alaouite dynasty.

He married Lala Latifa, whose family can trace a long line throughout Moroccan history. They have five children. The oldest is Crown Prince Sidi Muhammad, who was born on August 21, 1963. The prince eventually will succeed Hassan as king.

When he was four years old, Sidi Muhammad made his first visit to the United States and attended many ceremonial functions. He made his first public speech when he was only six! He talked about distributing land to the farmers. In 1975, he led the Moroccan delegation to the coronation of King Juan Carlos I of Spain. The prince speaks French and Arabic and is studying English.

A MIXTURE OF LAWS

Moroccan law is a mixture of traditional Islamic law, the French and Spanish legal systems, and Berber customs. Legal confusion can arise because there are differences between the religious laws and the civil code. Morocco's Supreme Court is divided into five chambers, each responsible for specific duties. For instance, the criminal division handles only criminal appeals. The constitutional division discusses matters dealing, of course, with the constitution.

The parliament is now called the Chamber of Representatives. Members are chosen for four-year terms. There are 306 members in the Chamber. Two thirds are chosen by voters and one third is elected by unions, professional associations, and commercial groups. Every Moroccan twenty-one and over is required to vote. Moroccans take their voting responsibilities very seriously and most turn out on election day. The legislative elections held in September of 1984 had a voter turnout of over 65 percent.

In 1971, the country was divided into seven administrative regions, each consisting of several provinces. The provinces are headed by governors. The country's two major cities, Rabat (the capital) and Casablanca, are called prefectures. Their pashas act as governor and mayor; they are appointed by the king. The smaller cities are administered by elected councils.

In the mid-1980s there were twelve political parties in Morocco. Five have been formed since 1979. Each party reflects different political outlooks; all exist and work within the framework of the constitution. The oldest is the Istiqlal party. It was formed in 1944.

Under King Hassan II, Morocco takes its international responsibilities seriously. The country is a member of the United Nations, the League of Arab States, and the Organization of African Unity.

Thus, after centuries, Morocco has finally been stabilized.

Above: Rabat, the capital of Morocco,
      is situated on the Atlantic coast.
Left: A decorated door in
      the old section of Rabat

Chapter 5

LAND OF

IMPERIAL CITIES

Rabat ★

Morocco's past can be studied in its cities. The history of this ancient land is written in the architecture, the life-styles, and the history of its towns. Morocco is not just endless vistas of desert sand, but a bustling, busy country. It combines the modern with the traditional. Over the centuries, four cities were capitals. They are now called imperial cities: Rabat, Fès, Marrakech, and Meknès. Each is beautiful, with an old district surrounded by the stark trappings of the new and modern.

RABAT—A ROYAL SPECTACLE

Rabat has been the capital since 1913. Moulay Youssef, who became sultan in that year, moved the government from Fès, where it had been for hundreds of years. He thought Morocco needed a fresh start, away from the political corruption that flourished in Fès. Rabat is now one of the largest cities in Morocco.

It is one of the four imperial cities of Morocco, located on the left bank of the Bou Regreg River. The north side of the city stretches along the Atlantic Ocean. There are many good beaches there for vacationers. Rabat is the center of transportation in

The Royal Palace in Rabat

Morocco with two railway stations and a major airport. Highways lead here from all parts of the country.

The city's main street is called the Avenue Mohammed V. It is barely two miles (three kilometers) long, running from north to south. Rabat is quiet, filled with flowers and trees. Although it is small, Rabat has had a long and important history. It was built by the Oudaias in the tenth century, but ruins of an ancient Roman town have been uncovered there as well.

From its strategic position on the Atlantic Ocean, Rabat was the launching point for the *jihad*, or holy war, against the Christians in Spain. It eventually became a hideout for the Moriscos, the Spanish Muslims. They became pirates after being expelled from Spain in the 1500s. After the city was brought under the control of Moulay Ismail in the 1670s, Rabat lost its importance, becoming a sleepy trading center.

Left: Walls and cannon of the old palace in Rabat. Right: Rabat's landmark, the Tower of Hassan, was built at the end of the twelfth century.

That all changed when Rabat became Morocco's capital. Everywhere there are new buildings, government and business workers in suits, and many cars and buses. But visitors can still see the pink walls of the fort that surrounded the old Casbah. The Museum of Muslim Art in Rabat, near the main gate into the Casbah, has the finest collection of Berber items in the world.

The city is known for its rug makers and jewelry designers, whose shops are everywhere.

Rabat was once a military center. It was called "The Camp of Victory" during the Spanish wars. There are ruins of fortifications throughout the city.

The Tower of Hassan is the most impressive. It was built between 1195 and 1199 by Yacoub el Mansour as part of a huge mosque in which his entire army could pray. The tower is 144 feet (44 meters) high, with walls 8 feet (2 meters) thick.

Members of the Garde Royale at the Tower of Hassan

King Muhammad V is buried near the tower. The mausoleum and mosque of Muhammad V rise from a white marble terrace. Four members of the Garde Royale watch over his tomb.

It is exciting to be in Rabat on a Friday. This is the day the king leaves his chambers in the Royal Palace for noon prayers in a nearby mosque. He is preceded by a parade of the Garde Royale. This hand-picked, well-trained bodyguard unit is made of scarlet-coated descendants of West African slaves brought to Morocco three hundred years ago by Sultan Moulay Ismail. Water sellers are everywhere, some giving drinks to the soldiers.

The king is dressed in white robes. He rides to the mosque in a coach pulled by four horses. On all sides are members of the Garde Royale cavalry. The clip-clop of hooves echoes over the stones in the street. The spectators applaud, which is the Moroccan form of cheering. The king's prayers are broadcast through loudspeakers to the people in the outside courtyard.

Before the king leaves the mosque, handsome horses, each a different color are led to the mosque. Beautifully dyed wool blankets lie across their saddles. Doctors of Koranic law, also dressed in white, who have been praying with the king, leave the mosque. They line up for the return procession. The coach, now empty, and the cavalry get in line. Finally, the king leaves the mosque. He rides a white horse and is shielded from the sun by a huge parasol. This is truly a royal spectacle!

Across the Bou Regreg River from Rabat is the city of Salé. The Hassan II bridge spans the river, yet some tourists still like to take the little ferryboats that scurry like water bugs from bank to bank. Built by the Romans, Salé eventually became the chief port and trading center of medieval Morocco.

Its residents were great sailors who enjoyed a bit of piracy once in a while. Robinson Crusoe had a run-in with "Salee rovers" at the start of his adventures.

Once a giant water gate stretched across the harbor mouth. Ships could pull in there during storms, where they would be safe. True to their heritage, the Salé boatmen annually hold a major festival on the eve of Mouloud, the birthday of the Prophet. They parade through the streets, carrying intricately carved candles.

FÈS—CENTER OF LEARNING

The oldest of the imperial cities, Fès, was founded in A.D. 808 by Idris II. It was originally a trading center and became the Moslem intellectual capital by the ninth century A.D. Fès is still a major commercial city. There are several colleges in Fès keeping alive the Muslim heritage of learning. The most important school is

Fès is surrounded by hills.

Qarawiyin University, one of the oldest universities in the world. It was founded in A.D. 859. Islamic students from all over the world come here to study.

Near the university is the Souk of the Carpenters. An elaborately carved gate is over the entrance to an ancient caravanserai located in the souk. A caravanserai is a combination inn, warehouse, and camel yard where caravans could stop for a rest. Today, the building houses poor students.

The tombs of the ancient Moroccan rulers, the Merinides, are on a high hill overlooking Fès. The view from the hill is one of the most beautiful in Morocco, especially at sunset. The colors of the city seem to glow in the dusk as the setting sun strikes the white, pinks, and greens of the buildings and towers.

The former imperial palace in Fès covers more than two hundred acres (eighty-one hectares), consisting of buildings, gardens, and courtyards. The medina (old city) is huge. The winding streets are so confusing that no first-time visitor should attempt to wander them alone. But one can always follow one's nose to find the tannery quarter. The smell of drying skins and dye vats is certain to lead you back to the same spot!

It is easy to get lost in the narrow little streets in the medina of Fès (left) but not hard to find the tannery quarter (above) because of the odor.

Meknès, with its decaying walls

MEKNÈS—ONETIME MILITARY BASE

Meknès once was another capital in Morocco's past. It is located on a plateau of the Middle Atlas Mountains. More than twenty-five miles (forty kilometers) of triple walls and hundreds of towers run around its perimeter. The city was the military base for Moulay Ismail in the 1600s. Hundreds of years later, the French followed his example and made it one of their principal army camps.

Moulay Ismail's imperial palace was built by slaves. Most of them were Christian seamen captured by his fleets in the Mediterranean. He was a very cruel ruler. One story relates his favorite method of execution—the victim was sliced in half from the head down. When Moulay Ismail died, he left more than five hundred heirs. Each could legitimately claim the Moroccan throne. Many of his sons demanded to be made sultan. In the ensuing confusion, Meknès was attacked several times and damaged heavily. Subsequently, it lost most of its importance.

A great variety of items can be found in the market in Marrakech.

MARRAKECH—SHOPPERS AND FOUNTAINS

The fourth imperial city, Marrakech, was founded in the
eleventh century by the Veiled Men, fierce mounted warriors
from the Sahara. They used the city as their headquarters
throughout all their wars. Underground tunnels built then still
carry water to the fields ringing the city.

Marrakech's vast city square, called the *Jemaa el Fna,* is *the*
meeting place of Morocco. Its name means Assembly of the Dead.
That is a grim title for the liveliest souk in the country. It probably
got the name from the days when the caliphs displayed the
severed heads of their enemies.

The square is always crammed with small stalls selling every
imaginable item. Weaving in and out of the crowds of shoppers
are porters who carry raw materials and finished products to and

Beautiful gardens can be found in Marrakech (above). In Jemaa el Fna Square one can see monkey shows (right), performing acrobats (below right), and crowds of shoppers (below left).

from the craft workers' shops. During the morning, the barbers are very busy, shaving the heads of the camel herders.

The warrior-tribesmen are bald, except for a single lock of hair. It is believed that when a Muslim soldier dies for his faith, Allah will grab that lock of hair and pull him into paradise!

By noon, the storytellers, musicians, and dancers fill every open space. There are snake charmers, fire-eaters, sword swallowers, and acrobats as well. They are paid by spectators who toss them coins. When all these acts are going on at once, the noise is tremendous.

The market finally quiets down in the evening, when the muezzin calls the faithful Muslims to prayer. He stands in the minaret, the tower high above the mosque, and chants in a singsong voice that can be heard for miles. In the olden days, the muezzin had to depend on the power of his lungs. Today, many use loudspeakers.

The Koutoubia, 203 feet (62 meters) high, towers over the city. Built in the twelfth century, it is covered with elaborate geometric and floral patterns.

Marrakech is a city of fountains, which are used to water livestock and for drinking. It is also a city of gardens, much like Rabat. The sultans who lived here loved planting trees and flowers. The handiwork of their slaves and gardeners is everywhere. Many gardens date from the twelfth century. The most famous is Agueda, with olive and other shade trees irrigated by a series of pools.

Just outside the town walls is a vast parking lot for almost every means of transportation imaginable. It is packed with carts, donkeys, horses, camels, trucks, cars, buses, and wagons.

Casablanca is Morocco's commercial and industrial capital.

CASABLANCA AND TANGIER

But there are other cities just as fascinating as the imperial four. Casablanca, one of the most famous, in one of the world's busiest ports and the hub of Moroccan commerce. For years it was one of the few places open to non-Moroccan traders.

There are many seaside resorts and nearby hotels that attract European visitors. Casablanca ("The White House" in Spanish) is only about sixty miles (ninety-seven kilometers) southwest of Rabat, the country's capital. But the differences between the two cities are easy to see. Where Rabat is peaceful, Casa (as it is nicknamed) is bustling. Casablanca is "where the action is." It no longer has that exotic movieland image once given to it by Hollywood. It is a brassy, loud, modern city.

Many poor people from other parts of Morocco have moved to

Most people living in Casablanca rely on the port (left) for their livelihood. The old medina in Casablanca (right) has narrow streets and whitewashed buildings.

Casablanca, hoping to find jobs. The government is trying to help them by building housing. Yet it is hard to keep up with the demand.

Casablanca is a maze of narrow, short streets that seem to branch off in every direction. Visitors need a guide to get through the town. But the Place des Nations Unies, in the city center, is a beautiful spot and easy to find. Many palm trees and flowers are planted there. Nearby is the Municipal Theater, the Central Post Office, the town hall, and the courts. Street vendors are everywhere, hawking their wares.

Residents of the city are sports crazy. They seem to enjoy everything. The Marcel Cerdan Stadium is used for rugby and soccer matches. World famous bicycle racers enjoy the Velodome. Horse racing, tennis, golf, and sailing are also popular. There is even a mountaineers'club in Casablanca!

Left: Casablanca's City Hall
Right: The Casbah in Tangier, the old Arab residential quarter

People who have visited Casablanca say that the city combines the best and worst of everything: lovely scenery and hardworking people versus poverty and crowded living conditions. Yet the Casablancans are very proud of their ancient heritage and believe that somehow everything will work out all right.

Tangier is the principal town in the north. When Moulay Ismail set up his court in Meknès in 1703, he kept the Christian envoys cooped up in Tangier. He therefore indirectly started the tradition that Tangier was an international center. In fact, after World War I, the 140 square miles (363 square kilometers) covering the city and its suburbs were designated just that—an international zone. A council looked over the concerns of the city. Six Moroccan Jews, six Berber Muslims, and representatives of Belgium, Spain, France, England, Holland, Italy, and Portugal directed the daily workings of Tangier.

Tangier is a city of contrast. Some people still use donkeys to
carry their belongings (left) while others use sleek boats (right) for pleasure.

Only in 1956, when Morocco became independent, did Tangier
revert to the country's control.

True to Tangier's international flavor, there is a collection of
seventy thousand toy soldiers on display in the Palais Mendoub
on Rue Shakespeare. The value of the exhibit is estimated at $1
million! The soldiers depict troops from many nations. Most of
the tin-lead alloy figures are very old.

In the olden days, travelers had a perilous journey to the
harbor. First they would have to climb down a ladder from their
steamship and scramble into a longboat. This was dangerous,
especially if the sea were rough. The longboat would carry the
travelers closer to shore where a mob of shouting porters would
scurry out from the wharf. The visitors would then crawl into
chairs held by the porters, who would wade through the surf to

Tangier is a favorite stop for tourists in Morocco.

land. Sometimes, if the visitor didn't tip enough, he might be dumped into the water. Tourists are happy that it's easier today. The harbor has been deepened and the fancy cruise ships can come alongside the dock. It's simple to walk down the gangplank to shore. But it's certainly not as colorful.

The Morocco of Tangier is much like southern Spain, because of the influence of the Moors in both areas. The old section of the city could be lifted from a province just across the Strait of Gibraltar. Today, the city is very modern and progressive. It has become the showcase of Morocco, with its highly developed tourist industry. It's been that way since the Phoenicians rowed toward shore more than two thousand years ago. They were probably greeted by the ancestors of those old-time porters. Do you think they were carried to land as well?

THE EDGE OF THE SAHARA

There are few cities along the edge of the desert. The harsh landscape and climate have prevented much large-scale growth, although there are ancient villages and small forts, called *ksour*

A Blue Woman (left) from the Goulimine area. The white-roofed building in Tinerhir is a holy man's tomb.

(*ksar*, singular), dotting the oases. Trails and roads connect the towns. Zagora is one of the last towns in Morocco outside the 1,000 miles (1,609 kilometers) of open desert.

However, some of Morocco's best scenery is along the rocky, sandy countryside of the south. The Blue Men live there. The hair, skin, and beards of these nomads have turned blue because of the indigo-colored dyes used in their clothes. The rich oasis called the Tafilalet is a collection point for caravans of the Blue Men coming and going across the desert.

There are other important border cities as well. Hundreds of traders attend the huge Sunday camel market in Rissani. Tinerhir was once an important outpost for the fabled French Foreign Legion. Goulimine is at the very edge of the sand, like a post at the edge of the ocean.

Morocco's cities, towns, and villages are important for its people. They provide a sense of security in an ever-changing land.

Water sellers, in traditional costumes and carrying shining copper cups, can be found in most markets.

Chapter 6

FROM SOUKS TO PHOSPHATES

Morocco has a mixture of old and new. The souk, or market, is where the average Moroccan shops. But beyond the souk is the modern world of international loans, investments, mineral resources, and research. Morocco is proud of both.

THE SOUK: HEART OF THE NATION

The souk is basic to the Moroccan life-style. The majority of Moroccan people live in the country; the market gives them a chance to meet old friends, stock up on supplies, and have some fun.

In the towns, souks are open every day. The craftsmen are organized according to their trade. There is a carpet souk, a goldsmiths' souk, and many others.

The market has always been the heart of the Moroccan town. Craftsmen long ago formed guilds, or trade associations. Each has a chief and a *mohtasseb,* or provost, who settles disputes that might arise between guild members. The *mohtasseb* is a very important figure in a souk. He controls the quality of merchandise and food, ensures that the scales used to weigh goods are accurate, and performs many similar duties. A souk might be busy and confusing to non-Moroccans, but native Moroccans are used to the uproar.

The main souk in a city is called the *kissaria*. This term dates back to ancient Rome. A *kissaria* is protected by heavy walls and massive gates. It is usually used as a warehouse for expensive goods. Many guards, belonging to the porters' union, patrol the walls at night. In addition to carrying goods around the marketplace, porters are also responsible for security in the smaller souks.

The vendors lay out their wares: tea, spices, beautiful hand-embroidered gowns, candles, peanut oil, tools, slippers, books, vegetables, or other products. Bartering is part of the tradition of the souk. With every lively discussion over price between a shopper and a seller, a smiling crowd gathers to see who will come out on top. It's all in good humor. Both sides will be pleased with the final bargain. Often, at the conclusion of a deal for more expensive items, the vendor will offer the customer some mint tea.

Early in the morning of a rural market day, tents and stalls are put up in the open country or in an enclosure where various tribes traditionally have met. The market is usually along a trade route near a major crossroad. The country souk runs for a week, usually once a month, depending on the size and economic importance of the area it serves. The rural souk is divided into sections. On one day, cereals and grains will be sold; on another, livestock. The market is named for the day on which it is held: *Souk el Khemis* (Thursday market), *Souk el Had* (Sunday market), and so on.

The most important country souks are the huge livestock

Left: A Berber carrying a sheep bought at the market at Imilchil
Right: Bartering at the wool market

markets at the edge of the Sahara. The Goulimine camel market is one of the largest in North Africa.

CARPETS, COPPER, AND CRAFTS

Moroccan crafts are known worldwide for their beauty and texture. Carpets are among the most popular items made in Morocco. The government closely checks the quality of each carpet. The price is determined by the square meter (about ten square feet).

The Moroccans have always raised sheep, which produce the wool used to make carpets. Wool is considered good luck, so weavers always tie a few strands in their headdresses to keep away evil spirits. Sometimes, a wool bracelet is placed around a horse's leg if the rider is traveling over rough country. He hopes the wool strand will protect the animal from injury.

Expert craftsmen make the colorful rugs of Morocco.

The Moroccan carpets are very colorful. The wool is dyed in traditional red, blue, white, black, yellow, orange, and green hues and shades. Family patterns have been handed down for generations. The colors used in a particular carpet identify the tribe that made it.

Leather workers are highly respected in Morocco. There are tanners in every city. They use huge outdoor vats filled with the chemicals used to treat the animal hides. The place where the tanners work is easily identified—the smell is terrible!

The leather is made into many items: saddles, sandals, knapsacks, book covers, purses, and chairs.

Another important craft material is copper. Dishes, plates, trays, pots, and goblets are handmade from this metal. Ironwork is also very beautiful, especially in railings, mirror frames, and lamp stands. On the more delicate side is embroidery—tablecloths, shawls, and seat cushions. Pottery and woodworking are still very popular in Morocco, as well.

Left: A stall with copper products in the souk
Right: Dyers' souk in Marrakech

The silversmiths are very proud of the sheaths they make for the huge, curved daggers carried by Moroccan men. The intricate inlay often takes months to perfect. The *mukka*, or long-barreled musket used by Moroccan warriors, is also set with precious silver. The trigger guard and stock are usually the most ornate parts of the weapon.

Today's Morocco is more than just a country with rural markets dealing in handicrafts. In the 1980s, King Hassan initiated an $18-billion national development plan that created one million jobs. The country has received financial help from the United States, European nations, and the Arab states. Since it is the world's oldest Islamic monarchy, Morocco is considered stable and a secure investment risk.

A SEARCH FOR MINERALS

Phosphates are Morocco's chief mineral resource. Reserves of the rock are estimated at sixty billion tons (about fifty-five billion metric tonnes). This is at least 75 percent of the world's supply. Phosphates are used primarily for fertilizers. The Office Cherifien des Phosphates (OCP) is responsible for overseeing the export of this valuable commodity. The general director of OCP travels around the world to negotiate the best prices. In the mid-1980s, the Moroccans were earning $4 billion annually in profits from the sale of phosphates.

A subsidiary of OCP, Fertima, produces fertilizers in eight new plants in Morocco. The country hopes eventually to be able to convert much of its phosphates into finished products. In that way Morocco can get the most profit from its most extensive natural resource. OCP employs 26,000 persons, making it the largest single enterprise in the country.

It is very expensive to import oil for energy use. Since Morocco wants to be more self-sufficient, much of the nation's economic development money is being used to build hydroelectric dams and to search for coal and gas reserves. The Moroccans are also hoping to eventually use the estimated twenty billion tons (about eighteen billion metric tonnes) of oil shale found underneath their land. The oil shale needs special production techniques to make it usable, so it will be a while before this resource can be exploited.

FARMING AND FISHING

In 1981 and 1982 Morocco was affected by the worst drought it had experienced in thirty-five years. Crops withered and died.

Left: Fruit, especially oranges, for sale in Casablanca
Right: Threshing grain

People lost their jobs. It was a very difficult time.

However, the rains returned in the winter of 1982. The country gave its thanks to Allah and headed back to the fields. The land is productive again, although Morocco still must import about 1,000,000 tons (907,200 metric tonnes) of grain a year. However, Morocco exports many agricultural items, such as green beans, peppers, eggplants, avocados, and strawberries. Moroccan wine is also exported, mostly to the Soviet Union.

Markets are being sought everywhere for Moroccan farm products. For instance, exporters are hoping to persuade foreign purchasers to buy clementines, which are Moroccan oranges, instead of Japanese mandarin oranges.

Independent fishermen carry their catch on their bicycles.

Morocco has become more independent in food production. Twenty years ago, the country had to import all its sugar. Today, Morocco produces 60 percent of its sugar needs. In addition, it has built refineries at Gharb and Loukkos, each of which can process 4,000 tons (3,639 metric tonnes) of raw sugar a day.

There are still some farming problems that need to be overcome. Many Moroccans use small, inefficient plots of ground on which to raise crops. The government hopes that eventually larger, more productive farms can be used. More mechanization is also required to help with the planting and harvesting.

Fishing remains largely undeveloped, although Morocco has an extensive coastline near some rich Atlantic beds. A Ministry of Fisheries was created in 1981 to coordinate dock construction and help to locate catches scientifically. There are about 28,000 independent fishermen. They row their small boats just offshore, usually catching sardines, which are important to the Moroccan diet. A new fleet of power boats and a canning industry are being planned.

Modern day "pirates" have been raiding the Moroccan fishing

Passengers board a Royal Air Maroc jet at Casablanca airport.

areas, much to the dismay of the small operators. Russians, Japanese, Koreans, Cubans, and Spaniards have been accused of poaching an estimated $1 billion worth of fish annually from the waters claimed by Morocco.

Moroccan industry is still in its infancy. However, plants manufacturing chemicals, textiles, machinery, and electronic equipment are now operating. Foreign investment is encouraged to finance and build these facilities. Many French, Italians, Russians, Americans, and Rumanians are helping with construction projects.

TRANSPORTATION AND TOURISM

To serve Morocco, the country has improved its 31,000 miles (49,879 kilometers) of roads, 1,151 miles (1,852 kilometers) of railroads, and nine international airports. There are two national airlines: Royal Air Maroc is the international carrier and Royal Air Inter runs domestic flights.

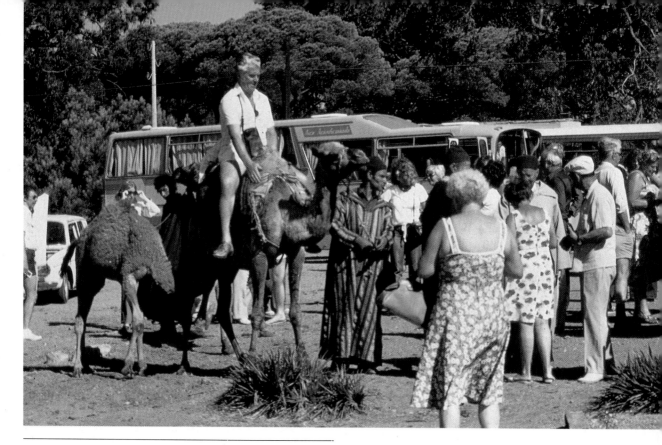

Tourists can take bus trips to see different sections of Morocco and if they want, they can take a ride on a camel.

Tourism has long been a key element in Morocco's economy. The country is close to Europe and is served by many foreign airlines. Every year French, West German, and American visitors flock to Agadir, a popular seaside resort city on Morocco's southern Atlantic coast. Agadir has been totally rebuilt since an earthquake destroyed it in 1960. The country's imperial cities of Rabat, Fès, Meknès, and Marrakech also are prime tourist attractions.

There are many holiday retreats along the coasts, including several operated by the internationally known Club Med, a French resort company. More than 1.5 million tourists annually vacation in Morocco, with a growing new market from other North African and Arab countries.

An international newsstand in Casablanca

On bright winter days, the beaches are crowded with visitors seeking suntans. Well-broiled tourists then move inside and enjoy the gambling casinos at Marrakech, Mohammedia, and Tangier. Golf courses being built at Rabat and other cities stand in great cultural contrast with the rural communities nearby.

COMMUNICATION: NEWS AND ENTERTAINMENT

Until 1936, publication by Moroccans of Arabic-language newspapers was not allowed. The French and Spanish, who ruled the country prior to that time, were worried that such publications might undermine their authority. A few Arab journals were allowed in the late 1930s, under the condition that they advocate moderate political views. However, the independence-minded Moroccans still managed to print underground papers, despite the restrictions.

Today, publishing is a thriving business in Morocco. Most newspapers represent political parties, each with widely differing viewpoints on how the country should be run. Freedom of expression is guaranteed by the constitution, but some editors were jailed during the emergencies of the 1960s and 1970s.

Al Anba, the Arabic language daily paper, is published by the Moroccan Ministry of Information. It is considered the official voice of the government. *Al Alam*, owned by the Istiqlal party, is probably the largest privately owned newspaper, with a circulation of about forty thousand. There are also many foreign-language papers circulated in Morocco, most of them imported from France.

The Maghrib Arab Press, the official news agency, supplies news to overseas radio and television stations, newspapers, and magazines. It has reporters in all major Moroccan cities.

Radio and television are closely controlled by a government agency called Radio Maroc, an agency of the Ministry of Information. Shows are broadcast mostly in Arabic and French, but there are Spanish and English radio programs at various times. It is possible to receive television programs from Europe.

Morocco is now manufacturing television sets, although they are too expensive for the average Moroccan to buy. Many sets are owned by community groups or cafés, where people can come to watch. The government also has given free sets to youth hostels.

Moroccans love movies. They enjoy American westerns, French comedies, and Egyptian love stories. Most of the theaters are in the bigger cities; for instance, Casablanca has at least fifty. The Ministry of Information also operates mobile theaters that visit

An advertisement for a movie

oases and small villages. There are not too many places in the world where nomads on camels travel to town for a night of watching movies!

Some movies are made in Morocco. Many are documentaries that display the rich spread of the country's cultural life. However, most major films are imported.

Morocco is slowly moving further into the worldwide economic community. It has a great many important products to offer. As such, it is seen as one of the most important countries of North Africa.

The original North Africans
were Berbers. Many Berbers,
and their descendants, still live
in Morocco. Above: A group in the
countryside. Left: A woman in the
souk. Below: Children from
the northern slopes of the
Atlas Mountains near the
town of Midelt.

Chapter 7

NOTES ON THE MOROCCANS

Most Moroccans are descended from Berbers or from the Arabs who invaded the country during the Muslim conquests. There are also twenty thousand Jews living in Morocco, plus an ever-changing small population of black nomads called the Harratines, who are a desert tribe.

The population of Morocco is over twenty million. Most people live west of the Atlas Mountains in the more fertile regions.

TRIBAL LIFE-STYLES

Arabic is spoken in the cities and along the seacoasts, with Berber still the native language in the remote districts. Almost all Moroccans can speak several languages. French and Spanish are easily understood by most people in the cities.

The Berber life-style centers around the tribe. Everyone in a

A moussem *is held in Tan Tan in May. Camel racing and dancing are part of the festivities.*

tribe can trace his family back to a common ancestor. So last names begin with the prefixes *beni* or *ait*, meaning "sons of." There are at least six hundred different Berber tribes.

Often disputes arise between the tribes. Mediating these arguments are the marabouts, who are combination judges, holy men, prophets, and homegrown saints. They must also be very brave, since they sometimes have to step between two warriors slashing at each other with knives.

The marabouts also perform another important service. By following their example, other Muslims learn how to live good lives. When a marabout dies, his tomb is often considered a holy place.

An annual pilgrimage to these tombs is called a *moussem*, an important event in the life of a religious Berber. Over the centuries, huge fairs have grown up around these pilgrimages. One of the largest is El Aouina Moussem, about eleven miles (eighteen kilometers) from Marrakech. Almost three hundred horsemen take part in the fantasia, or cavalry charge, which is usually part of the festival's excitement.

A man pours tea for his guests as his child watches.

Another *moussem* is held annually the third week in September in Imilchil, a small village in the High Atlas Mountains. By tradition, all engaged couples from the area are married on that weekend. In ancient days, a marabout had blessed the weddings of neighborhood young people. Ever since, couples have been coming to Imilchil on pilgrimages, hoping to receive the same blessing. Usually, more than thirty thousand people assemble for two days of dancing and singing.

Religion is very important to Moroccans; it is part of their daily life if they are Muslim. In addition to the marabouts, other religious leaders are important in Moroccan society. The *alem* teaches Muslim law. The *khatib* preaches sermons. The muezzin calls everyone to prayer. The *hezzab* reads the Koran, the Muslim holy book. These are not clergy because there are no priests or ministers in Islam. But they are highly respected in the community and what they say is strictly followed.

Factory workers in Marrakech

URBAN WORKERS

Urban influence has steadily been chipping away at the rural customs and practices of both Berbers and Arabs. Many young Moroccans have adopted European manners and styles.

Yet it is necessary to keep some tribal ties, even when living in a large city. It is sometimes important to know someone in order to get a job. Often whole sections of factories are staffed by members of the same tribe. They were hired by a relative or recommended by someone from their home village who had moved to the city years earlier.

Some tribes specialize in certain kinds of work, even if they live in the city. For instance, many of the Zenata are waiters; the people from the Tiznit plains are said to be expert electrical workers.

Cannery workers

The Ministry of Youth, Sport, Labor, and Social Affairs is responsible for enforcing laws pertaining to workers. Moroccans are supposed to be paid a minimum wage, but the amount varies in different parts of the country. A social security system covers about 20 percent of the laborers, mostly those in industry. Disability payments and pensions are also paid.

In the loneliness of the cities, workers often join unions, both for the companionship and to protect their rights.

The largest labor organization is the Moroccan Labor Union, which has about 800,000 members. It includes workers in mining, transportation, railroads, and public works. Next is the Union of Moroccan Workers, with about 150,000 members—mostly teachers and port laborers. The unions have become stronger in recent years, bargaining for higher minimum wages, housing allowances, and other benefits.

Some Moroccan women still wear veils in public.

Women in Morocco have always held a special place. Even though many still wear veils and often don't meet with male guests, the women are important. They are not considered inferior. There is a Moroccan saying that the man rules the family but the wife rules the man. Through long tradition, the head of the house is responsible for his mother, aunts, daughters, and servant women and their families. He often takes the women's advice very seriously.

Moroccan schoolchildren learn in their history books that Youssef ben Tachfin became the head of the Almoravids because of the support and encouragement of his wife, Zeineb.

It is not out of the ordinary today to see Moroccan women in professional and governmental positions. For years, they have had the right to vote.

Berber schoolboy reading Arabic from the blackboard.
Arabic is read from right to left, not left to right.

A HERITAGE OF LEARNING

Expanding the educational system is a primary goal of the
government. Under the French protectorate, only a few
Moroccans were able to attend schools. Arabic was taught as a
foreign language! Young children had to attend classes in a local
mosque to learn Islamic theology, speaking skills, and Arabic
grammar. Since independence, Morocco has had a lot of catching
up to do.

When Muhammad V returned from exile in 1955, he demanded
the founding of a school to train teachers. He knew this was
necessary to help Morocco move ahead in the modern world.
After this was accomplished, a Higher Council for National
Education and the National Council for Culture were formed.
These two groups advise the minister of education on school

Boy scouts and their friends

problems. As a result, the building of schools increased, free
education was instituted, scholarships were started, and more
teachers were recruited.

Currently, more than 1.5 million young Moroccans attend grade
schools. However, many children drop out within five years. They
are needed on the family farms or to help with the family
business. Almost one fourth of the secondary school pupils drop
out before graduation.

Most children attend two years of preschool. They learn about
their Muslim faith and practice writing, addition, and subtraction.
After that, they have five years of primary school and must take
an exam before moving on to secondary school.

There are four basic years of secondary school, followed by a fifth year of specializing in science, the humanities, or some sort of technical training. Two more years—called the baccalaureate—follow, with emphasis on natural sciences, science, math, humanities, and economics. After graduation, the Moroccan student can look for work, move on to a university, or receive more technological training.

All through history, Moroccans have loved higher learning. Even the lowly Moorish peasant respected and admired the scholar. The nation's poets, scientists, and scholars were active when most of Europe was wallowing in the Dark Ages. In fact, the writings of ibn Rushd or, as he is better known in the West, Averroes (1126-1198), kept alive the ideas of Aristotle, the famous Greek philosopher. Because of their geographic location and their organizational skills, the Moroccans—the Moors of old—influenced much of the world. Even as they conquered, they brought culture.

The sultans surrounded themselves with wise men who were experts in history, farming, and medicine. Their courts had skilled glassmakers who could devise telescopes. Their metalworkers studied the strengths and weaknesses of steel and subsequently made excellent weapons.

While some Europeans believed that foolhardy sailors would eventually drop off the end of the world, Moroccan geographers and explorers were mapping vast regions of Africa. In 1550 one even drew the first map of Russia.

The Muslim religion contributed to this skill. Once in his or her lifetime, each devout Muslim is supposed to visit Mecca, the holy city of Muhammad. Even during daily prayers, the people face that revered site in Arabia. It was thus necessary to be very

People who have not learned to read and write can use the services of a public writer.

accurate in pinpointing Mecca from every direction. As a result, pilgrims could travel and the faithful could pray.

Arab numerals, still used in mathematics, were perfected by the Moors. They also added greatly to our knowledge of algebra and astronomy, in addition to developing the decimal system.

The thousand-year-old Qarawiyin University in Fès is a legacy of all this. However, at the beginning of independence, only a few hundred Moroccan students attended the university. But by 1975 more than 75,000 were enrolled in various institutes and schools established almost from nothing.

Schools were built in Rabat and Fès, and later in Casablanca, Marrakech, and Oujda.

PROJECTS AND PLAY

All their lives, young Moroccans are taught the value of their heritage and the importance of helping to build a new nation.

Boys coming home from school stop for an impromptu game of soccer outside the old city walls in Marrakech.

Everyone was excited when independence finally arrived. In the 1950s, more than ten thousand youngsters helped build a "road to unity" linking northern and southern Morocco. Even Crown Prince Hassan worked on the highway. Another project led by young Moroccans involved the planting of 900,000 trees to fight erosion.

But young Moroccans love to play as well. Soccer, or football, is considered the most fun. The national government has built many stadiums and soccer fields, in addition to those built by cities. An empty lot can also serve as a field. In any village, youngsters playing ball are a common sight.

Swimming and gymnastics are popular in school. Well-to-do Moroccans can afford a great time skiing in the Atlas Mountains.

The Moroccans are fiercely proud of their past. They know they can draw on all the resources of a rich tradition to help them in today's fast-paced world.

An Andalusian musician plays the classical music of Morocco.

Chapter 8

PEOPLE OF MUSIC
AND CULTURE

The Moroccan has a keen ear for music. Whenever a nomad caravan stops at an oasis for the evening, someone will pull out a bendir drum, a circular wooden frame covered with hide. A companion will rummage in his pack for a flute or a single-stringed rebab, which is shaped like a fiddle. Thus will start a desert music session—unplanned, improvised, and intriguing.

The music bounces toward the stars, in a lilting, wild strain of sound that was old when the Arabs met the Berbers for the first time.

Moroccan musicians are revered for their skill, whether they play a lute or tambourine. Musical art is very important in Morocco's national culture.

The music of the cities is different from that found in the countryside. Over the generations, it has become mostly instrumental. In rural areas, music is part of the folklore—which means it accompanies a story or a poem.

There are several major forms of Moroccan music. The first is the classical, or Andalusian. It is primarily chamber music played by men for men in the very traditional Moroccan society.

It is complicated, with lyrics sung in Arabic or the Andalusian dialect from Spain. It takes many years of studying theory and techniques at conservatories in Rabat and Marrakech to master this form. The music originated in Arabia and moved eventually to Damascus, then Baghdad, where it was perfected. Following the conquest of Morocco by the Omayyads, it eventually made its way to Spain in the ninth century.

After the fall of Cordoba, when the Spanish pushed the Moors back to Morocco, many refugees settled in Tlemcem, Fès, and Tétouan. They brought their music with them.

Andalusian music is regularly played by the National Broadcasting Orchestra and is presented in concerts. The Association of Anadalusian Music preserves this tradition by recording and writing down the scores.

Popular music, called *griha,* is more varied. It is designed to entertain the person in the street. This is the music of the souks. In the *griha,* long folkloric poems are recited, bringing alive the history of Morocco.

Another form, the *aita,* is sung as a prelude to dances. The *casida* is also popular. It is like a ballad, accompanied by a stringed instrument.

New songs are always being composed. Sometimes they are funny, sometimes sad.

DANCES AND DRUMS

Berber music varies according to the tribe. The songs are

A flute player leads the dancers as they perform the ahidou.

inspired by the Berber's laws of nature and landscape. They often tell of the day-to-day lives of the people. This music often accompanies dancing.

Moroccans are afflicted with dance fever. They love to dance. A typical dance of the Middle Atlas Mountains is the *ahidou*. Both men and women take part, standing shoulder-to-shoulder in a circle and clapping their hands and stamping their feet in special patterns. A musician called the *amessad* acts as conductor.

The Cheuhs enjoy the *ahouache*. In this dance, the men are the musicians and singers, while the women dance. Usually only the bendirs, the round drums, are used. The *ahouache* is often performed around campfires at night, which makes it very exciting and mysterious.

Accomplished acrobats

The Blue Men in the Goulimine region are noted for the *guedra*. The *guedra* is actually a drum, consisting of a skin stretched over the open mouth of a jar. The drum, which gives its name to the dance, is played with the fingers and the palm of the hand. Usually this dance is performed by one woman; Westerners might call it a "belly dance."

Another interesting dance originated in black Africa and is performed by descendants of the Negro slaves. There is much leaping and bounding, accompanied by drums and other percussion instruments.

The acrobats in *Jemma el Fna* souk in Marrakech perform in time to music. They are especially noted for their leaping and building of pyramids with their bodies. Moroccan acrobats have their own tumbling school at Amizmiz, near Marrakech. From there, many have performed all over the world, coming back to their villages when they retire.

A young woman dressed for the Feast of Sheep

HOLIDAYS AND FESTIVALS

Festivals provide plenty of excuses for singing and dancing. Among many others, there is the spring Cherry Festival in Sefrou, a Rose Festival at Kelaa des N'Gouna at the end of May, and the Equestrian Festival at Tizza—near Fès—in the first week of October. The king attends many of these events. One of the highlights is the annual Feast of Sheep, held at different locales around Morocco. King Hassan awards prizes to the best breeders, which are considered a great honor for the mountain shepherds.

Among legal holidays, Morocco marks its independence with a two-day celebration on March 2 and 3. November 18 is Independence Day, when Muhammad V became king. Religious holidays include Aïd es Séghir, the end of the fast of Ramadan; Aïd el Kebir, "The Great Feast" in commemoration of Abraham's sacrifice of a ram to God; the Mouloud, the anniversary of the

Prophet Muhammad's birth; and Achoura, the tenth day of the Muslim new year. The dates of the latter depend on the Muslim calendar.

On Mouloud, children go from house to house greeting all the neighbors. The lucky youngsters get presents. Firecrackers are set off everywhere.

All the adults are glad when the fast of Ramadan ends. During the month-long fast, adult Muslims must go from 5:00 A.M. to 8:00 P.M. every day without eating or drinking, although water is allowed. So Aïd es Séghir is welcomed with relief.

FOOD FIT FOR A FEAST

The hospitality of the Moroccan is legendary. Even strangers are honored guests in a Berber or Arab home. Whenever anyone visits a home, a hearty meal—the *diffa*—is provided. The fancier restaurants and wealthier families often emphasize French-style cooking, a holdover from the days of the French protectorate. The ordinary people have simpler food, usually a thick soup called *harira*, with tomatoes, peppers, and olives, and bread made from barley flour.

On feast days, the *bastilla* is prepared. It takes all day to get it ready. For a large party, 104 thin crusts of baked pastry are used as dividers between layers of chopped pigeon meat, sugar, almonds, and many other goodies. Of course, it is eaten only on very special occasions.

The *tajine* is a stew made from chicken, pigeon, mutton, or beef. The meat is cooked for hours to make a soup base, to which are added olive oil and spices. The result is something like a heavy gravy, so thick it can be eaten with the fingers.

The bastilla *is eaten on special feast days.*

Mechoui is roast mutton, usually a whole sheep broiled over an open fire. Sometimes, the sheep is placed in a huge oven and cooked overnight.

The head of the house always pronounces a blessing before anyone begins eating. Once the ritual is completed, the food is passed. Traditional Moroccans usually eat with their right hand. They scoop the first three fingers into the pot and bring out a piece of meat. Bread is used to soak up the sauce. If a Western visitor is invited to a Moroccan home, utensils are usually provided the guest to avoid embarrassment.

Many meals conclude with *couscous*. This is boiled grain, flavored with spices or sweetening. Be careful of *couscous* with red peppers. It can set your mouth on fire!

Moroccan pastries are usually sweet and sticky, made with lots of honey. Moroccans, as Muslims, are not supposed to drink alcohol. They seldom drink liquids during a meal, except for a sip

Left: Flat bread cooked in a village oven in the Tessaout Valley of the Atlas Mountains. Right: Selling brochettes in the desert near Tan Tan.

or two of water. Before or after eating, they might drink orange juice. Almond milk, made from crushed almond nuts, is a very rare treat and is very expensive. But wealthy Moroccans enjoy having this delicacy available for their guests.

Tea is the principal beverage after meals. The host often presents an elaborate ceremony of mixing tea, mint, and sugar. It is fun to watch. The tea is slowly sipped and it is impolite not to have at least three cups.

Since Morocco is a seacoast country, it is easy to find many fish recipes. The French brought in their love of sauces, which the Moroccans now use in abundance with seafood. Kabobs are also popular. These are skewers with meat of various kinds that are roasted over glowing charcoal.

Left: Closeup of the intricate carving on King Hassan II's private mosque. Right: An entrance to an apartment building in Casablanca with colorful tiles and stone carving

HOUSING

Older Moroccan houses are usually behind high walls. Gardens and patios greet the visitor who passes through the front gate. The airy, open spaces make a surprising contrast after coming in from a crowded, narrow street. Moroccan architecture is known worldwide for its ornate decorative style called arabesque.

Younger people are building more modern homes, often where there is space at the edge of the cities. These, as well as the homes in the very poorest sections of town, are certain to have little gardens.

Plain or fancy babouches *can be found in just about any color.*

Everyone removes his or her shoes when entering a Moroccan house. Slippers, called *babouches*, are worn inside. They can be very ornate or very simple, depending on the taste of the wearer. Outside, most of the men wear typical Western business suits. However, to protect their clothes from dust and rain, they might wear a loose-fitting robe called the *djellaba* as a coverall.

LITERATURE AND DRAMA

In their leisure time, modern Moroccans enjoy reading. Moroccan authors write both in Arabic and in French. Many of their stories deal with the birth of their nation, the status of women, and questions of culture. Driss Charibi is a well-known author whose works in the 1950s and 1960s were about the problems of a Moroccan living in France. Ahmed Sefrioui has been highly praised for his stories about the peasants and craftsmen in his country.

Other important Moroccan authors include Muhammad Khair

A play performed outdoors in Tinerhir

Eddine, Muhammad al Sabbagh, Bel Hachemy Abdelkader, and Abdulhamid Benjelloun, who write in Arabic. They have won many literary prizes and the Moroccan people are proud of them.

The storytellers in the souks come from a much more ancient cultural tradition. Moroccans of all ages and social classes love the tales of Jeha. He is portrayed as a clown; everyone wants to take advantage of him. But Jeha is very wise and always outwits the villains. Other stories tell of good and evil spirits that are believed to roam the mountains and the plains. A storyteller can talk for hours, accompanied by a drum.

The French introduced drama to Morocco. Theatrical companies began touring, aiming mostly at audiences of the European community and Moroccans who were educated overseas. After independence, many amateur theater groups sprang up. They dealt with problems between modern youth and traditionalist parents, economic difficulties, and similar subjects. A Moroccan National Theater was established in 1956 and a dramatic arts school was opened soon afterward in Rabat.

Plays are now performed either in French or Arabic.

Fès is Morocco's most important intellectual, cultural, and religious center.

Shakespeare's works are very popular, as are those of the classic French playwright Molière. In the souks, wandering comedians and mime artists draw large crowds. Their satire and acting are common to every society.

A LONG HISTORY

Moroccans see themselves as leaders of a group of moderate Third World countries. They are cultured and refined people, who now prefer mediation to warfare. There are some problems with the rebel Polisario from the Western Sahara region given to Morocco by Spain in 1976, but generally the borders are now fairly quiet.

Relations with the United States are friendly. They date back to 1777, when the sultan recognized the government of the new American country. Treaties of 1787 and 1836 are still in force, making it one of the longest, continuous foreign relationships in United States history.

The use of a flag as a symbol of state dates to the Almoravid dynasty (1061 to 1106). A white silk banner inscribed with verses from the Koran was given to every unit of one hundred soldiers. The Alaouites, dating from the seventeenth century, introduced the red flag. In 1912, the French put a green star in the center, to distinguish it from other red flags. King Muhammad V, as a descendant of the Alaouites, retained that design for the flag of the new Morocco.

Thus, the flag symbolizes the long movement of an old country into modern times. Combined with the flavor and culture of ancient heritage, it helps Morocco take its place in today's world.

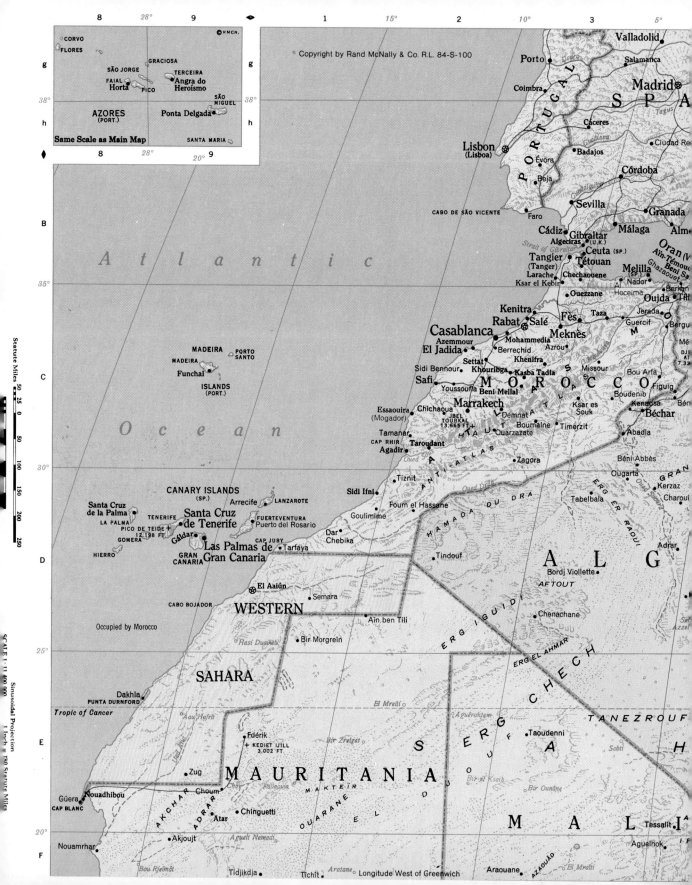

MAP KEY

Agadir	C3	Figuig	C4	Ouezzane	C3
Al Hoceima	B4	Foum el Hassane	D3	Oujda	C4
Azemmour	C3	Goulimime (Goulimine)	D2	Rabat	C3
Azrou	C3	Guercif	C4	Rhir, (Cape)	C3
Beni Mellal	C3	Jbel Toubkal, mountain	C3	Safi	C3
Berguent	C4	Jerada	C4	Salé	C3
Berkane	C4	Kasba Tadla	C3	Settat	C3
Berrechid	C3	Kenitra	C3	Sidi Bennour	C3
Bou Arfa	C4	Khenifra	C3	Sidi Ifni	D2
Boudenib	C4	Khouribga	C3	Oued Sous, river	C3
Boumalne	C3	Ksar el Kebir	B3	Strait of Gibraltar	B3
Casablanca	C3	Ksar es Souk	C4	Tamanar	C3
Ceuta	B3	Larache	B3	Tanger (Tangier)	B3
Chechaouene	B3	Marrakech	C3	Tarfaya	D2
Chichaoua	C3	Meknès	C3	Taroudant	C3
Dar Chebika	D2	Mellilla	B4	Taza	C4
Demnat	C3	Missour	C4	Tétouan	B3
Oued Drâa, river	D3	Mohammedia	C3	Timerzit	C4
El Jadida	C3	Oued Moulouya, river	C4	Tiznit	D3
Essaouira (Mogador)	C3	Nador	B4	Youssoufia	C3
Fès	C3, C4	Ouarzazate	C3	Zagora	C3

*Above: Steel rods
ready for shipping
at Casablanca's port
Left: Shopping in a souk*

MINI-FACTS AT A GLANCE

GENERAL INFORMATION

Official Name: Kingdom of Morocco

Capital: Rabat

Official Languages: Arabic and several Berber dialects. French is often used in business, government, and schools above the primary level.

Government: Morocco is a hereditary, constitutional monarchy. The king is the head of state. He appoints the prime minister and cabinet ministers and presides over the cabinet. The legislature, called the Chamber of Representatives, has only one chamber, whose 306 members are elected for six-year terms. The government is divided into three branches—executive, judicial, and legislative.

Morocco has thirty-one provinces and two urban prefectures (cities). The Supreme Court is the highest court and there are regional courts and three courts of appeal.

The king has broad powers of government. He can dissolve the Chamber of Representatives and dismiss cabinet members and the prime minister. He can also declare a state of emergency.

The Moroccan constitution, adopted in 1972, gives the people of Morocco freedom of speech, movement, and the right of assembly. There are two major political parties, the *Istiqlal* and the Socialist Union of Popular Forces.

Religion: Islam is the state religion. However, there are about seventy thousand Christians, mostly Roman Catholic, and twenty thousand Jews.

Flag: The flag has a five-pointed green star at the center of a red background.

National Song: "Al Nachid Al Watani" ("The National Anthem")

Money: The main monetary unit of Morocco is the dirham. The dirham is divided into 100 centimes. There are coins of 5, 10, 20, and 50 centimes and 1 and 5 dirhams. Bills are issued in 5, 10, 50, and 100 dirhams. As of January 1984, 8.16 dirhams equaled one U.S. dollar.

Weights and Measures: Morocco uses the metric system.

Population: 22,495,000 (1984 estimate)

Cities:

Casablanca	1,506,373
Rabat	367,620
Marrakech	332,741
Fès	325,327
Meknès	284,369
Tangier	187,894

(Population based on 1971 census)

GEOGRAPHY

Highest Point: Djebel Toubkal, 13,665 ft. (4,165 m) in west central part of the country

Lowest point: Sea level along the coast

Coastline: Atlantic, 612 mi. (985 km); Mediterranean, 234 mi. (377 km)

Mountains: The Rif Mountains and the Atlas chain predominate. The Atlas is divided into the Great or High Atlas region, the Middle Atlas, and the Anti-Atlas. One third of Morocco is mountainous.

Desert: The southern border of Morocco ends in the vast unmarked Sahara Desert.

Rivers: The major rivers in Morocco are the Moulouya, 320 mi. (515 km) long and the Sebou, 180 mi. (290 km). There are also the Grou, the Bou Regreg, the Oum er Rbia, the Ziz, and the Dades.

Climate: Morocco is known for its basically hot and sunny climate. But it can be very cold in the mountains, and the Atlantic cools the coastal area. The capital of Rabat has an average of 81° F. (27° C) in the summer and 45° F. (7° C) in the winter. Marrakech, in the interior, has more extreme temperatures—an average of 101° F. (38° C) in the summer and 40° F. (4° C) in winter.

It rains in the north between November and April. The northwestern Atlas Mountains have about 32 in. (81 cm) of rain a year, while the desert gets less than 8 in. (20 cm). There the average temperature in summer is 130° F. (54° C) and 62° F. (17° C) in winter.

No matter where one lives in Morocco, "sirocco" winds sometimes roar in from the Sahara. These are hot and very dry winds that bring choking clouds of dust.

Greatest Distances: Morocco stretches 760 mi. (1,223 km) from east to west and 437 mi. (703 km) from north to south.

Area: 254,816 sq. mi. (659,970 km²)

Trees: The trees in Morocco are similar to those in Spain and Portugal. In the mountains there are cedars, firs, and junipers. South of Essaouira there is the tropical argan tree. Other prevalent trees include the cork oak, evergreen oak, and the thuja (a pine). In arid areas one finds wild olive, mastic trees, dwarf palms, and date palms.

Fish: Offshore fishing is considered good, but underdeveloped in Morocco. Main catches include sardines and lobster.

Animals: Common animals include domestic animals such as sheep, goats, horses, and camels. Wild boars are often found in the more remote regions. Hyenas, jackals, and foxes are the largest meateaters in the wilds. Barbary apes, barbary sheep, porcupines, and hedgehogs also live in the mountains. White vultures, hawks, owls, and storks are common birds of prey. Puff adders and Egyptian cobras can be found around rocks and caves.

Birds: There are many birds. White vultures, hawks, eagles, and owls help control the rodent population in the countryside. Pigeons and other birds that are good eating are everywhere. So are sparrows and ravens.

EVERYDAY LIFE

Food: A typical Moroccan dinner consists of a thick soup called *harira,* which is eaten with tomatoes, peppers, olives, and a bread made from barley flour. A simple meal usually suffices unless a guest is present. Then a heartier meal called the *diffa,* is prepared. It can range from roast mutton to lemon-flavored chicken. Many meals conclude with *couscous,* which is boiled grain mixed with sweets or hot red peppers. Desserts are rich and made with honey.

On feast days, the *bastilla* is prepared. It is a dish that takes all day to prepare. Thin crusts of baked pastry are used as dividers between layers of chopped pigeon meat, sugar, almonds, and many other ingredients.

French food is served in elegant restaurants and in wealthy homes. This custom is a holdover from the days when Morocco was a French protectorate.

The Moroccans who are Muslims are not supposed to drink alcohol. They seldom drink during a meal, except for a sip or two of water. Before or after eating, they might drink orange juice or tea. Almond milk, made from crushed almonds, is a rare treat and very expensive, but is drunk by wealthy Moroccans.

Housing: Homes in Morocco may be hundreds of years old. They are usually constructed of adobe and have high walls to protect the privacy of the families. Many have no windows in order to reduce heat. They crowd up against the narrow streets and are entered through large gates. Inside are gardens and patios that are bright and airy.

Some poor Berbers in cities live in primitive dwellings made of canvas, planks, and corrugated iron. Herdsmen live in wood huts or goat's hair tents.

Holidays:

January 1, New Year
March 3, Festival of the Throne, anniversary of King Hassan's coming to the
    throne
May 1, Labor Day
Beginning of Ramadan (ninth month of the Muslim calendar)
Aïd es Séghir, end of Ramadan
Aïd el Kebir, Feast of the Sacrifice (varies according to the Muslim calendar)
October 8, Muslim New Year
October 17, Achoura
November 6, Anniversary of the Green March
November 18, Independence Day
Mouloud, Birth of the Prophet (varies according to the Muslim calendar)

Culture: The audience for Moroccan literature is limited by the fact that many people are illiterate. There are two literatures to choose from — Arabic and French. Although French has predominated in modern times, a modern Arabic literature is beginning to emerge. Two dominant themes in modern Moroccan literature are the birth of the nation and the status of women.

Among the most famous Moroccan authors are Driss Charibi, whose best works, written in the 1950s and 1960s, deal with the problems of a Moroccan living in France. Ahmed Sefrioui has been highly praised for his stories about peasants and craftsmen in the country. Other important Moroccan authors include Muhammad Khair Eddine, Muhammad al Sabbagh, and Bel Hachemy Abdelkader.

The French introduced drama to Morocco, but it was mainly aimed at the European community and Moroccans educated overseas. A Moroccan National Theater was established in 1956 and a dramatic arts school was opened soon after in Rabat. Theater is subsidized in Morocco. Plays are performed in French or Arabic. Shakespeare and Molière are very popular.

Folk arts are very important in Morocco. Every spring there is a folklore festival in Marrakech. Music is part of the folklore, which is to say that it is used to accompany a story or a poem.

There are several major forms of Moroccan music. One is called classical or Andalusian. It is primarily chamber music played by men for men in traditional Moroccan society. There are lyrics that go with this music sung in Arabic or the Andalusian dialect from Spain. Conservatories of music are located in Rabat and Marrakech.

Moroccans love to dance. A dance native to the middle Atlas mountains is the *ahidou*. It is a circle dance in which men and women take part. Another famous dance is the *guedra*. The *guedra* is actually a drum and it is used to accompany one woman who performs what we know in the West as belly dancing.

There are many festivals held in Morocco in which singing and dancing play a part. For example, there is the spring Cherry Festival in Sefrou, a Rose Festival at Kelaa des N'Gouna at the end of May, and the Equestrian Festival at Tizza — near Fès — in the first week of October.

The entrance to the Royal Palace in Rabat

Architecture is one of Morocco's best-developed arts. Its roots go back to Roman time. However, the predominant patterns of Moorish architecture were set in the eleventh and twelfth centuries. Moroccan buildings, which are very ornate, show the influence of Syrian, Byzantine-Syrian, and Andalusian elements.

Sports and Recreation: Moroccans love to play ball. Among the most popular sports are soccer, basketball, field hockey, and volleyball. Swimming, gymnastics, and boxing are also favorite pastimes as are track and field. In the 1984 Los Angeles Summer Olympics, for example, Morocco was the only African country to win two gold medals. Said Aouita, the 5,000-meters world record holder and Olympic gold medalist, is a national hero.

Communications: There are around eight daily newspapers in Morocco and thirty-five weekly and monthly magazines. *Al Anba,* the Arabic language daily, is the official newspaper of the country. It is published by the Moroccan Ministry of Information. There are many other papers in the country, most published by political parties. The Maghrib Arab Press is the official news agency. Radio Maroc oversees operations of radio and television stations. In 1982, there were about 2,500,000 radio receivers and 823,000 television sets.

Transportation: There are about 30,000 mi. (48,000 km) of improved highways in Morocco. Less than one third are paved. Motor vehicle registrations number about 300,000. About two thirds of that number are private autos. Most motorists who own their own cars live in the north or in the cities. Morocco also has more than 1,000 mi. (1,600 km) of good railroads. There are nine international airports and about thirty airfields. Royal Air Maroc is the international airline owned by the government. Royal Air Inter manages domestic flights. The chief ports of Morocco are Casablanca, Safi, and Mohammedia.

Schools: There are two years of preschool education, during which children learn the fundamentals of the Muslim religion and are introduced to reading and mathematics. Five years of primary school and five years of secondary school follow, the last year of which children specialize in science, technical subjects, or the humanities. Two more years of higher level work are next before university training begins.

Morocco faces a number of problems in educating its people. Only about 25 percent of its population is literate. Much of the population is young, the birth rate is high and there are a lot of differences among the various types of schools—French, Spanish, Muslim, and Moroccan government schools. Morocco spends about one quarter of its national budget on education.

Education is compulsory between the ages of seven and thirteen years old. In spite of this, only about 65 percent of school-aged children attend school. All primary teachers are Moroccan. Arabic is the language of instruction for the first two years of school and French and Arabic are used for the next three.

Secondary education may be given for three or four years, depending on the course of study selected. About 25 percent of these students attend technical schools. Most secondary school teachers are native, but many are from overseas, mostly France.

There are six universities and several other institutions of higher learning. The oldest university in Morocco is the Islamic University of Al Qarawiyin at Fès which is over 1,000 years old.

Health: All workers in Morocco pay into a Social Welfare Fund, which is an insurance program for sickness, accidents that happen at work, and old age. In rural regions, there is a high mortality rate.

ECONOMY AND INDUSTRY

Principal Products:
Agriculture: Wheat, citrus fruits, sugar beets, wool, almonds, barley, beans, olives, corn, and oats
Manufacturing: Textiles, electronic equipment, candles, cement and other building equipment, foodstuffs, and leather
Minerals: Phosphates, coal-oil shale, limestone, marble, clay, and lead

IMPORTANT DATES

12th century B.C.—Phoenicians visit Moroccan coast

5th century B.C.—Carthaginians trade with Berbers

146 B.C.—Carthage defeated by Rome

33 B.C.-A.D. 44—Morocco ruled by Rome as kingdom of Mauretania

3rd century A.D.—Roman influence declines

A.D. 622 — Start of the Muslim calendar

A.D. 632 — Death of Muhammad

682-3 — Arabs under Oqba ben Nafi invade Morocco

701 — Moussa ibn Nusair invades Morocco

710 — Morocco converted to Islamic faith

711 — Moors (Moroccans) invade Spain

808 — Fes founded by Idris II

10th century — Political confusion

1062-1070 — Marrakech built by Youssef ben Tachfin

1082 — Morocco unified

16th century — Moors driven from Spain

1672 — Moulay Ismail becomes Sultan

1777 — Sultan recognizes the new government of the United States

1801-05 — Barbary Wars

1817 — Piracy outlawed in Morocco

1830 — France seizes Algeria and makes it a colony

1871 — Algerian rebels defeated

1906 — European conference to determine if a European power should control Morocco

1907 — French move into Casablanca

1911 — Spain sends troops into Morocco

1912 — Tangier becomes an international zone; French protectorate begins

1920s-34 — Rif War against France and Spain

1927 — Sidi Muhammad ben Youssef becomes sultan

1934 — France gains complete control of French Morocco

1939 — World War II begins

1942 — French Morocco becomes a major Allied base

1953 — Ben Youssef and his family exiled

1955 — French bring ben Youssef back from exile; an independent monarch is established

1956 — France grants independence to Morocco

1957 — Sultan Muhammad V takes the title of king

1958 — Spain turns over most of Spanish Morocco to the Moroccans

1961 — King Muhammad V dies; his son becomes King Hassan II

1962 — Morocco adopts first constitution

1963 — First Moroccan parliament

1965 — Student-led riots in Casablanca; state of emergency declared

1970 — New constitution approved

1972 — New constitution approved; Hassan suspends the legislature

1975 — Moroccan "Green March" — over 300,000 people march into Spanish territory to claim district for Morocco

1976 — Spain gives lands in Western Sahara to Morocco and Mauritania; Polisario revolt begins

1979 — Mauritania gives up its claim to Saharan territory; peace treaty signed with Polisario; territory claimed by Morocco

1980s — Conflict over Western Sahara continues; domestic unrest prevails

1984 — King Hassan signs treaty of union with Libyan leader Col. Muammar el-Qaddafi.

1986 — Israeli Prime Minister Shimon Peres meets with King Hassan in Morocco. Libyan criticism leads to King Hassan's ending the treaty of union with Libya.

IMPORTANT PEOPLE

Mahjoubi Ahardane (1922-   ), one of the founders of the Mouvement
  Populaire
Driss ben Omar al-Alami (1917-   ), general, one of Morocco's important
  military leaders

Muhammad Allal al-Fasi (1906-1973), founder and head of Istiqlal party

Ahmed el Mansour (1578-1603), leader of the Saadian dynasty

Emperor Augustus (63 B.C.-A.D. 14), Roman emperor

Averroes (Rushd ibn, Abu al-Walid) (1126-1198), physician and writer, known for his writings on Aristotle

Muhammad ibn Abd Allah ibn Battuta (13-4-1377), geographer and travel writer

Caligula (A.D. 12-A.D. 41), Roman emperor

Driss Charibi (1926-   ), novelist and short story writer

General Rodrigo Diaz de Vivar ("El Cid") (1043-1099), Spanish military leader killed by the Almoravids

King Ferdinand II (1452-1516), Spanish king who drove the Moors from Spain

Hassan II (Prince Moulay Hassan) (1929-   ), current king of Morocco

Ibn Khaldun (1332-1406), historian, philosopher, sociologist, and politician

Idris II (791-828), founder of the city of Fès

Queen Isabella I (1474-1504), queen of Spain and wife of Ferdinand II

Juba II (50 B.C.-A.D. 24), Berber king

Kahena (-696), Christian or Jewish woman guerrilla leader who harassed attacking Arabs during the Muslim conquest

Kosaila (-688), Christian Moroccan prince who resisted Arab invasion

Marshall Louis Lyautey (1859-1934), French soldier who saved Morocco from Germans in World War I

Moulay Ismail (1642-1727), second king of the Alaouites who restored order to Morocco with the help of black slave-soldiers and Europeans

Ibn el Qadi (1552-1615), scholar, poet, and biographer

Ibn Nusair, Moussa (640-714), Muslim governor of North Africa who led an invasion of Morocco

Muhammad (570-632), founder of Islam

Obeid Allah (-934), founder of the Fatimid Dynasty

Moulay Rashid (seventeenth century), first Alaouite ruler

Septimus Severus (146-211), Roman emperor between 193-211

Sidi Mohammed (1963-   ), crown prince of Morocco

Sidi Muhammad ben Youssef (-1962), first king of independent Morocco

Ibn Tufayl (-1185), philosopher and scientist

Muhammad ibn Tumart (1078?-1130), leader of the Almohads

Yacoub el Mansour (-1199), first builder of Rabat

Ahmed Sefrioui (1915-   ), short story writer

Youssef ben Tachfin (1061-1106), leader of the Almoravids, founder of Marrakech

Above: A spice dealer
Below: A Berber girl chats with her friend while she spins wool.

INDEX

Page numbers that appear in boldface type indicate illustrations

About the Author

Martin Hintz, a former newspaper reporter, has written more than a dozen books for young people. The subjects range from training elephants to other social studies titles included in the Childrens Press Enchantment of the World series. He and his family currently live in Milwaukee, Wisconsin, which he admits is a long way from Morocco. Hintz has a master's degree in journalism and is a professional travel writer/photographer who has won numerous awards for his work.

The author would like to express his special thanks for help in preparing this book to Abdelkader El Kadiri and the cultural affairs section of the Moroccan embassy, the Moroccan Government Tourist and Information Center, and Ms. Gloria Flowers of Royal Air Maroc.